BIRMINGHAM CITY TRANSPORT'S DEMONSTRATORS

DAVID HARVEY

AMBERLEY

Front cover: 159 JHX
The rather neat-looking 159 JHX was an AEC 'Regent' V with a Park Royal body and was built with an AEC 7.685-litre AV470 engine coupled to a four-speed synchromesh gearbox. It is working on the 14E route in Crossfield Road, Lea Hall. 159 JHX was demonstrated three times to BCT between June 1956 and April 1957, but on its final visit had a semi-automatic monocontrol gearbox. And it still failed to get an order! (L. Mason)

Rear cover: 9 JML
9 JML was the second Crossley-bodied Crossley 'Bridgemaster' to be built and was exhibited at the 1956 CMS. It was demonstrated to BCT in its green livery from February 1957 in order to test the feasibility of using a 30-foot-long and 8-foot-wide seventy-two-seater bus in Birmingham. From that point it was a success, but when buses were large orders were placed in 1963, although they were the same size and capacity they had rear engines. 9 JML was purchased in September 1957, becoming 3228 and is parked near to Lea Hall Garage still with the 'ON HIRE' sticker in the nearside front window. (D. Williams)

First published 2021

Amberley Publishing
The Hill, Stroud
Gloucestershire, GL5 4EP

www.amberley-books.com

British Library Cataloguing in Publication Data.
A catalogue record for this book is available from the British Library.

ISBN 978 1 3981 0672 7 (print)
ISBN 978 1 3981 0673 4 (ebook)

Typeset in 10pt on 13pt Sabon.
Typesetting by SJmagic DESIGN SERVICES, India.
Printed in the UK.

Contents

Introduction

During the period from 1913 to 1968, Birmingham's municipal undertaking had very stringent requirements and specifications for the buses they bought. Being the largest municipal operator in the United Kingdom, orders bus for chassis, engines and bodies were highly sought after by vehicle manufacturers and many of them supplied buses for inspection and trial on routes. In addition, buses were exhibited at the pre-war Olympia and post-war Earl's Court Commercial Motor Shows from a batch of buses in order to obtain further orders from elsewhere. This book shows both the successful and unsuccessful demonstrators and examples of the follow-up orders.

History

During its fifty-five years operating bus service in Birmingham, the City Transport Department had, over the years, many buses on loan from prospective chassis and body-building manufacturers in an attempt to obtain orders from the largest municipal operator in the United Kingdom. Orders from Birmingham required that manufacturers met very specific requirements of the General Manager's staff, who at once were very mechanically forward-thinking but conservative in their body styling and requirements for passenger comfort. On the plus side, BCT were pioneering operators of top-covered double-decker buses. In November 1922 twelve Railless F42 trolleybuses with Roe H25/26RO bodies for the new Nechells route were introduced, while bus 101 (OL 8100), an AEC 504 with a top-covered Brush H26/24RO body, entered service on 24 July 1924. After two experimental six-wheelers – 208 and 209 of 1926 and 1927 respectively, which had closed-in staircases – in October 1929 the first enclosed driver's cab AEC Regent 661, 338 (OF 3970), entered service with an internal straight staircase, a large rear platform, a comparatively low seating capacity, generous leg room and lots of internal polished wooden fittings. These all became the Birmingham standard layout until the end of half-cab double-deck purchases in 1954. BCT buses now had moquette upholstery and leather cloth upper saloon seating, with the comment being made in a trade journal that riding on a Birmingham bus one had the choice of 'the lower saloon lounge or the upper saloon gentlemen's smoking room'. On the negative side the buses were always 7 feet 6 inches wide, which restricted seat and gangway widths. Even after 8-foot-wide bodies were permissible after 1950, saloon heaters were not entertained and doors on rear-entrance double-deckers were an encumbrance, despite nearby Midland Red having produced rear-doored buses since 1949. Mechanically, diesel engines were experimented with from 1930 in order to achieve better fuel economy and this was enthusiastically adopted as standard from 1934. The combination of a fairly light metal-framed bodywork, a small but reliable frugal diesel engine and a Wilson preselect gearbox (preferably from a West Midlands manufacturer) was the basis for all the pre-war orders for new buses up to 1940.

The result was that Daimler supplied 796 COG5 double-deckers and thirty-five single-deckers were delivered, starting with the first one, 564 (AOB 564), entering service on 4 May 1934 and culminating with 1237 and 1238 (FOF 237–238) being delivered on 1 March 1940. Most of the bodies were built in Birmingham by Metro-Cammell; though 245 bodies, they were constructed in Smethwick by BRCW between 1934 and 1940 as they essentially only built bodies in this period for London Transport and Birmingham.

Daimler had not got the capacity to cope with the huge orders from BCT as well as their other orders from elsewhere, and in order to start the closure of the tram system the two routes to Dudley – one via Handsworth, West Bromwich and Great Bridge, the other via Dudley Road, Smethwick and Oldbury – a total of 135 buses were bought from Leyland Motors with a specially modified Titan TD6c chassis that was unique to Birmingham. All were delivered in 1938 and 1939. Eighty-five were fitted with MCCW bodies while the remaining fifty had Leyland bodies. Both types of bodies had seating capacities that, at fifty-two, were two less than the contemporary Daimler COG5s due the extra weight of their torque converter gearboxes.

The first buses allocated to Birmingham City Transport by the MoWT were four 8-foot-wide Daimler COG6s that were intended to be exported to Johannesburg, but due to enemy submarine activity in the Atlantic Ocean were offered to Birmingham. After those came eight 'unfrozen' Leyland Titan TD7s, of which six were intended for Western SMT. The wartime period rather put an end to the inspection of demonstrators, although a London Transport AEC RT type was on loan in March 1942. The only available buses for most of the wartime period were Daimler CWG5s, CWA6s and CWD6s with preselector gearboxes and Guy Arab Is and IIs. The chassis from Bristol were not offered to BCT. Between 1942 and 1946, sixty-five Daimlers and eighty-five Guy Arabs were delivered to Birmingham, and all of these wartime buses had MoS bodywork of varying quality. They were not long-lived, however, with all being withdrawn from PSV work by January 1951. Surprisingly, in view of the huge numbers of new post-war buses that would be needed once the decision to scrap both the still extensive tram system as well as the Coventry Road trolleybus routes, to get rid of all the wartime 'utility' buses and virtually all of the pre-war bus fleet, only one bus was demonstrated to the Corporation. Crossley Motors had offered BCT a demonstrator in 1939 but the Corporation had to wait until 1945 before the post-war prototype Crossley double-decker arrived, and as Crossley apparently had the capacity to construct both chassis and bodies quickly, an order was placed in 1946; although, with problems over engines and BCT's exacting requirements, the first bus did not arrive until May 1949. The main supplier of bus chassis to Birmingham before the Second World War was Daimler, with the alternative source being latterly from Leyland Motors. Neither could supply enough chassis in the early post-war period and so the availability of the 270 Crossleys was an added bonus. However, a variety of issues with Leylands caused BCT to begin to look elsewhere for an alternative manufacturer. After their experience with wartime Guys, a new model was specifically developed by Guys, so that virtually all the deliveries of buses from 1950 until 1954 of traditional 7-foot 6-inch-wide half-cab, rear-entrance buses came from Daimler or Guy. Body contracts went to Brush and MCCW then after 1949 to Crossley, which were to the usual strict BCT specification. Other bodybuilder's products were purchased from Leyland and Park Royal, which were their manufacturer's standard bodies but with added BCT internal fixtures and fittings.

It wasn't until 1952 that another pair of demonstrators, one each from Daimler and Leyland, were on hire – a pair of underfloor-engined single-deckers. By this time the management of BCT began to realise that the early post-war buying spree of new buses would soon have ramifications in the early 1960s when literally hundreds of double-deckers would be approaching the end of their second seven-year Certificate of Fitness and a large number of new buses would be required. The traditionally equipped bodywork requirements for BCT was now becoming prohibitively expensive, and with falling passenger numbers just beginning to encroach on the profitability of the undertaking and fuel costs beginning to rise buses with lighter bodies but with a greater seating capacity were going to be required. As a result of this the 'golden age' of BCT demonstrators was about to begin.

All the demonstrators tried out from 1955 until 1960 were operated from Lea Hall Garage on the 14 service to Lea Hall and Kitts Green. This route to the east of the city centre was considered to have every type of operating conditions, with hilly sections, faster suburban sections, a high ridership and a very frequent service. The first three demonstrators were a pair of AEC Regent Vs and a Daimler CVG6, which were all 27 feet 6 inches long by 8 feet wide and had seating capacities in the low sixties. However, it was soon realised that buses of this size were not looking into the future requirements of the Transport Department. In 1957, a 30-foot-long Crossley Bridgemaster was trialled and subsequently purchased in order to test the feasibility of a conductor being able to collect fares from seventy-two passengers. Once this was proved possible (rather than satisfactory for the poor overworked conductor) a further rear-entrance bus, this time a Daimler CVG6-30, was tested. The final front-engined half-cab bus to arrive was another AEC Bridgemaster with a forward-entrance body, which stayed for thirteen months. Between 1959 and 1960 high-seat-capacity buses were trialled in the form of two of the advanced front-engined Guy Wulfrunian FDWs, two rear-engined Leyland Atlantean PDR1/1s and the prototype Daimler Fleetline CRG6LX. The commitment for front entrance, rear-engined, high-capacity double-deckers had been decided upon, and ten of each of the Atlantean and Fleetline chassis were bought for extensive comparison purposes. It was decided to purchase large quantities of the Coventry-manufactured Fleetline model with 576 double-deckers being bought, and this was the sole model of double-decker purchased by BCT until the end of municipal operation in Birmingham on 31 September 1969.

Throughout its existence, Birmingham always had a small fleet of single-deckers. In 1930 twenty Guy Conquest Cs were purchased, which were augmented in 1931 and 1933 by a total of fourteen Morris-Commercial Dictators. The final pre-war single-deckers were a total of forty-five Daimler COG5s delivered in 1935 and 1936, some of which were used to replace the earlier Guys. In 1950 thirty Weymann-bodied Leyland Tiger PS2/1 and five Leyland Olympic HR40s replaced the COG5s. By 1964 the half-cab PS2/1s, albeit fast, economical and comfortable, were coming towards the end of their lives and the conversion of thirteen of them to a one-man operation had not been a total success. Although twenty-four Daimler Fleetline CRG6LXs with single-deck Marshall B37F bodies were purchased in 1965, there was still a need for new single-deckers especially on the suburban 36 route, which had a very high ridership of factory workers in the peak periods but very few passengers during the rest of the day. In addition, BCT were introducing express services on some main arterial routes and although the 1950 Leyland Tiger PS2/1s were capable of a high speed and comfortable ride they were getting a bit long in the tooth so something more modern was required. It was against this backdrop in 1965 and 1966 that five single-deckers – a lightweight Bedford VAM5, an AEC Swift MP2R, a Bristol RELL6G, a Leyland Panther PSUR1/1R and a Daimler Roadliner SRC6 – were operated on the 20 and 27 single-deck services. As a result of these trials, rather perversely, twelve lightweight Ford R192s and two lengths of AEC Swifts entered service during 1967.

Between 1965 and the end of municipal operation a number of other buses were examined, but with the impending absorption into the new West Midlands PTE on 1 October 1969, no further demonstrators were operated. The Birmingham City Transport policies were largely carried over into WMPTE and the Daimler Fleetline, with either Metro-Cammell or Park Royal bodywork continued to be ordered.

1

The First Demonstrators and Resulting Buses: 1913–28

30 (KT 610) Tilling-Stevens TS3 40 hp, 325, Dodson O18/16RO, 9/1913
This Tilling-Stevens TS3 demonstrator was built in September 1913 for BMMO. It was re-registered OA 5711 during 1914. It had a Dodson O18/16RO body with a flush-sided body style known as an Allen type and it sat much lower on the chassis frame, with the rear wheels inside the rocker panels.

30 (KT 610)
In its original condition, Tilling-Stevens TS3 demonstrator KT 610 advertises itself when posed for an official photograph when still fitted with its low-height Dodson 18/16RO body. The bus was first operated by BMMO as a Tilling-Stevens petrol-electric demonstrator and was bought by them in 1914 and re-registered OA 5711. It was sold to Birmingham Corporation as part of the 1914 Birmingham Corporation Act along with twenty-nine other Tilling-Stevens buses. This agreement enabled Midland Red to operate into Birmingham while also protecting BCT fares. It became 30 in the Birmingham municipal fleet. (D. R. Harvey Collection)

TSM TS3 Tilling O28/22RO
This TSM TS3 double-decker was operated as a demonstrator from Tilling-Stevens between 11 March 1922 and 1 April 1922. No known photograph.

TC 2128, Leyland SG7 12462, Dodson O28/26RO, –/22
Originally registered TB 8886, this Leyland SG7 was on hire to BCT from 20 January 1922 to February 1922. Re-registered TC 2128, it was an early attempt by Leyland Motors to obtain an order from Birmingham. The open-topped Leyland SG7 model was fitted with a Dodson body styled to suit the requirements of operation in London and had an open, but full-width, cab in a semi-forward control layout. The demonstration was not successful and TC 2128 was soon purchased by United Counties of Northampton and given the fleet number C2.

TC 2128 is in Salisbury Road when working on the 1 route from New Street in the city centre to Moseley village with the conductor posing alongside the nearside front mudguard. The bus had a 40-hp petrol engine located behind a rather ugly looking 11-foot 'snout'. The Christopher Dodson open-topped body had the usual open rear staircase, but the seating capacity of fifty-four did rather point the way to the future numbers of passengers that could be carried. (D. R. Harvey Collection)

59 (OK 3980), AEC 503 503005, Fry O28/26RO, 26/12/1922

OK 3980 (59) was demonstrated for one month by AEC from 26 February 1922 until 26 March 1922, running on the trade plate 0033 HK, before it was purchased and given the fleet number 59. OK 3980 was originally built as a 403-type chassis but with a more powerful AEC 6.8-litre petrol engine. 59 was withdrawn in 1927 and sold to via ADC Limited, London, acting as a dealer, in June 1927. It then went to Cumberland Motor Services Limited, Whitehaven, as their 80 in September 1927 and withdrew it during 1930.

59 (OK 3980)

59 (OK 3980) was fitted with a body built by Fry of Greenwich and was the first new post-First World War BCT double-decker to enter service and the first in the fleet to have a forward control layout and a windscreen. It was an open-top fifty-four seater with an outside staircase, but by July 1924 it was obsolete as 101 (OL 8100), the first AEC 504 with an enclosed upper saloon, had been delivered. 59 is parked in Harborne Park Road when new in the spring of 1922. (BCT)

60 (OK 6364), AEC 403, 403007, ?, B32F, –/1923

61 (NO 6856), AEC 403, 403???, Dodson, B32D, –/1923
OK 6364 (60) was renumbered 80 in April 1923. NO 6856 (61) was renumbered 81 in April 1923. Both of these AEC 403-type single-deckers were on demonstration from AEC, Southall, between 27 March 1923 and 12 May 1923. No known photographs.

Enclosed Top Decks Arrive and Early AEC 504s

62 (OK 8004)
Above: Being tilt tested in Barford Street Garage in July 1924 is the one-year-old AEC 503 62 (OK 8004). Following on from the prototype Fry-bodied 59, one of the 60–71/89–90 class of Brush open-topped AEC 503 buses in 1923, 62 was experimentally fitted with a top cover following the successful precedence set by the top-covered Nechells trolleybuses introduced the previous year. Although it reverted to its original open-top condition after two months, it set the wheels in motion to order top-covered double-deckers from henceforth. (BCT)

109 (OM 208)
Below: The earliest production top-covered buses in the fleet were thirty AEC 504s with Short H26/26RO bodywork. They all had an outside staircase and an open driver's cab. Travelling along Yardley Road near to Augusta Road is 109 (OM 208), operating on the 11 route on 13 June 1934, having been fitted with pneumatic tyres some years before. 109 had entered service on 21 November 1924 and was withdrawn at the end of May 1935. (D. R. Harvey Collection)

111 (OM 210), etc.

Above left: Passing through Tyburn Road Works for the last time in around 1930 for its final overhaul is AEC 504 111 (OM 210), dating from November 1924. Separated from its Short H26/26RO body, the almost semi-forward-control nature of these chassis can be appreciated. 111 would be withdrawn on 31 July 1936. Behind it, having had its chassis and 6.8-litre petrol engine thoroughly overhauled as well, is a later ADC 507 that dated from November 1927. 280 (OX 1531) is waiting to be reunited with its Vickers H26/26RO body and sports the later ADC radiator badge. 280 was withdrawn on 31 July 1935. On the right are two early piano-front AEC Regent 661s and an almost new 7 (OF 6086), a 1930 normal control Guy-bodied normal control Guy Conquest C. (BCT)

177 (OP 206)

Above right: Travelling along Paradise Street when passing the Midland Institute building on the corner of Ratcliff Place, 177 (OP 206) is working on the Cross City 5 route from Sandon Road to Perry Common. Although it is not raining, it must have been a cold day as the driver of this open cab Short-bodied AEC 504 has pulled up the tarpaulin from beneath the cab cowling and pulled down the visor from beneath the front canopy. The top deck arrangement was very similar to that experimentally fitted to bus 62 with the upper and lower saloon body pillars not marrying up. (D. R. Harvey Collection)

208 (OP 237)

Opposite below: 208 (OP 237) spent the whole of its working life based at Harborne Garage operating on the then 4 route between New Street in the city centre and the Harborne terminus, which was adjacent to its home garage and adjustments so refuelling could take place. It is parked for a posed photograph in Edgbaston Park Road and clearly displays the sheer size of this 6-ton 11¾-cwt leviathan. The steep two-step entrance was something of climb but once inside the bus it had a flat lower saloon floor line. Running from the large enclosed rear platform is the staircase, which looked considerably safer than the then usual outside flight of steps. The body was sold as a caravan during 1935 and amazingly still exists in preservation. (BCT)

205 (OP 234)
Parked in Harborne on 15 October 1929 is 205 (OP 234), one of six AEC 504 powered by
an AEC 45-hp 6.8-litre petrol engine with a Birmingham-built Buckingham H26/26RO body
delivered in September 1926 and withdrawn at the end of July 1936. The bus would soon
become outdated with its outside staircase, a snout-like radiator projecting well forward of the
front axle and an open driver's cab, but it had been converted to operate on pneumatic tyres and
had by the standards of the day a long year service life. (J. Cooper)

Unsuccessful Six Wheelers

208 OP, 237 Guy BTX, BTX 22119, Short, H32/26R, 11/1926
This early Guy BTX was the last normal control double-decker to be supplied to
Birmingham, arriving on 1 November 1926. It had a Daimler-Knight CV35 six-cylinder
7.672-litre sleeve-valve engine whose engine oil consumption was prodigious and
whose reliability was very poor. 208 (OP 208) was fitted with pneumatic tyres from
new. The Short Brothers fifty-eight-seater body was the first in the fleet to have an
enclosed platform and staircase. It was withdrawn on New Year's Eve 1933 with the
chassis eventually becoming a lorry.

209 (OP 238), Karrier DD6 47004, Short, H32/28R, 8/1927

Another trial six-wheeled bus was 209 (OP 238). This was a forward-control Karrier DD6 with a Stafford-built Dorman 6JUL 6.9-litre petrol engine. The chassis was very heavy, unreliable and underpowered. There were also severe problems with the double-drive shafts and back axles, which resulted in a gruesome death of a female passenger in Wallasey in 1931. As a result of this incident, most six-wheeled Karriers were quickly taken out of service. 209 didn't even last that long because of its unreliability and was withdrawn after just two years' PSV service in November 1929. It became Service Vehicle 15 in May 1931 as a mobile crane lorry, but was replaced in January 1938 by the AEC Renown 663 bus 92 (MV 489)

209 (OP 238)

Left: 209 (OP 238) only had around three advantages over previous buses: it was fitted with pneumatic tyres, a totally enclosed driver's cab with a wonderful brass cab door handle and a fully enclosed rear staircase and huge platform. It could also carry sixty passengers but was so large for the period that no one knew what to do with it. As a result, it was used on the 34 route along Hagley Road to the Kings Head public house at Bearwood. It is parked prior to delivery on 28 April 1927 with the trade plate 123 CX. (BCT)

AEC 507s with Top Covers

229 (OP 7872)

229 (OP 7872), posed in front of Rochester Castle on 1 June 1927, was one of the earlier more powerful AEC 507 models bought by BCT, with a longer wheelbase of 15 feet 9½ inches. When new these Short-bodied low-height buses revolutionised the Inner Circle service, which had low bridges at Highgate Road and Icknield Street. Viewed from the nearside, the bodies gave the impression of having enclosed staircases, but they were actually outside. These AEC 507 chassis were delivered with pneumatic tyres and were the first buses in the fleet to have the driver's cab enclosed. The upper saloon had twenty centrally mounted angled single bucket seats and two side gangways. Because of this herring-bone seating arrangement they were known as the 'Pickpocket Specials'. (D. R. Harvey Collection)

209 (OP 238)

Opposite below: After conversion to a mobile crane and towing lorry as Service Vehicle 15, the six-wheel Karrier 209 OP 238 was used for recovery only as a last resort. It looked impressive, the only remnant from the original body other than the cab was the first bay, which contained a crew compartment. (BCT)

257 (OX 1523)
Opposite above: The nearside official BCT photograph of 257 (OX 1523), taken in October 1927, reveals that the design of the rear platform had been quite well thought out, with only two steps onto the platform itself before another step led to the lower saloon. The access to the enclosed upper saloon was exposed, steep and precarious, especially in the wet. 257, an ADC507 with a 6.8-litre AEC petrol engine, had a Short H26/26RO body with an enclosed driver's cab and pneumatic tyres. Entering service on 7 October 1927, it was withdrawn after just eight years on 31 May 1935. (BCT)

270 (OX 1546)
Opposite middle: The 13A bus route was first operated on 5 June 1929, so when ADC 507 270 (OX 1546) accelerated past the impressive portico of Birmingham's Council House in August 1929, leaving Victoria Square and passing into Colmore Row, the extended service to School Road, Yardley Wood, was still something of a novelty. Behind Victoria Square's ornate silver-painted gaslights, the passengers on 270's Buckingham-bodied top deck could have opened the windows to their maximum three-quarter drop position. (G. H. F. Atkins)

280 (OX 1531)
Opposite below: The development of the outside staircase ADC 507 continued throughout the latter part of the 1920s. In a congested New Street in around 1929 is 280 (OX 1531), a Vickers-bodied bus fitted with an enclosed driver's cab, which is working on the 13A route to Yardley Wood. The bus travelling in the opposite direction is 191 (OP 220), an earlier Short-bodied AEC 504 being used on the 6 route to Sandon Road. The rear view shows the rear platform and outside staircase layout. (J. Whybrow)

285 (OX 1570), ADC 507, 507068, Short, H24/26RO, 9/1927
Although not strictly a demonstrator, 285 (OX 1570) of June 1926 had the earliest of the AEC 507 chassis numbers in the BCT fleet. 285's Short body was constructed on very different principals, being one of the first metal-framed bodies built by the company. It was easily identifiable by having flush-sided lower bodywork without rocker panels. It was also the first four-wheel double-decker to be delivered with pneumatic tyres.

285 (OX 1570)
Right: Travelling along College Road, Moseley, when working on the 1A route between the city centre, Moseley and Acocks Green in around 1929 is 285 (OX 1570), the revolutionary all-metal framed Short-bodied ADC 507. Despite this the bus retained an outside staircase and was the last in the fleet to be delivered with an open cab. It was withdrawn in June 1937. (D. R. Harvey Collection)

286 (OX 4594), ADC 802, 802008, Short FH –/– RO (68), 1/1928
286 (OX 4594), was an Associated Daimler Company Limited demonstrator for
Birmingham Corporation Transport, which entered service in January 1928. Thirteen
of these unsuccessful six wheelers were supplied to London General (as their London
Six LS class), another chassis was never bodied and there were five demonstrators,
with one each going to Birmingham, Sheffield, Maidstone & District, Southdown and
Westcliff on Sea. OX 4594 was renumbered 100 in July 1928.

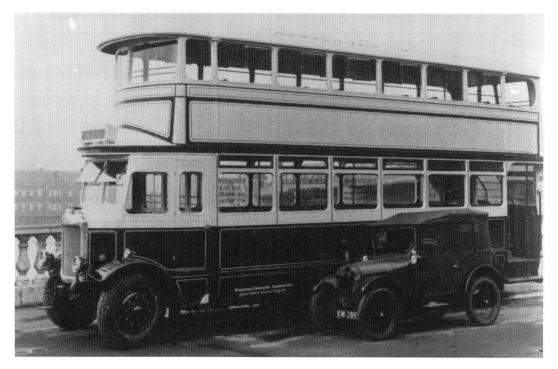

OX 4594
OX 4594 is parked alongside the River Medway in Rochester, Kent, near to the Short Brothers
factory when new in 1928. It was a poor chassis and had an even worse Daimler CV35 Mk I
5.7-litre sleeve-valve petrol engine. This bus was specifically built for Birmingham and had a
metal-framed, sixty-eight-seat body with a very modern-looking top deck, similar to the 1929
London General's six-wheeled LT type. By contrast the lower-deck saloon had old-fashioned
clerestory opening ventilators above the fixed-paned saloon windows. Yet it had a fully enclosed
rear platform and staircase, albeit reached by a rather deep second platform step and a full width
totally enclosed cab, which appeared to be tacked on to the rest of the body as an afterthought.
It remained in Birmingham until it was withdrawn on 28 October 1928. (Short Brothers)

TE 1128, Leyland Titanic TT1, 60004, Leyland, H40/32RO, 7/1927
This six-wheel double-decker bus was on demonstration from Leyland Motors Limited,
Leyland, during 1928. This vehicle was eventually operated by Western Scottish Motor
Traction, Kilmarnock, from 1932 until 1946.

2

Demonstrators Between 1928 and 1930

A New Breed of Double-Deckers

99 (OF 3959), Leyland Titan TD1, 70743, Leyland, L27/24R, 12/1928
OF 3959 (99) was a Leyland Motors Limited demonstrator, new in December 1928. It entered service with Birmingham Corporation Transport on 8 January 1929 with the Short H26/26RO body from OM 9573 (159), and ran with that registration and fleet number until June 1929 when the body was returned to the original 1925-built AEC 504 chassis. The TD1 returned to service as OF 3959 (99) with a Leyland L27/26R body on 29 September 1929 and purchased by the Corporation in February 1932. The original Leyland 6.8-litre petrol engine was replaced by an 8.1-litre diesel unit in June 1932. 99 was then sold to Preston Corporation in February 1935 after amassing just some 180,000 miles operating from Barford Street Garage.

99 (OF 3959)
Having turned into Coventry Road from Muntz Street 99 (OF 3959), the fifty-one-seat lowbridge Leyland-bodied Leyland Titan TD1 is working on the clockwise ring of the Inner Circle 8 route. The bus is crossing beneath the recently introduced Coventry Road trolleybus wires on the route to Yardley in 1934. Coming out of Golden Hillock Road is one of the Pickpocket Specials, a Short lowbridge-bodied AEC 507s. 99 was ideal for working on the Inner Circle route, which had two low railway bridges in Icknield Street and Highgate Road. The drivers generally liked driving the bus as it had a good turn of speed, but neither conductors nor passengers appreciated the lowbridge layout with its sunken offside gangway, rows of bench seats and limited headroom. (J. Whybrow)

MT 2114, AEC Regent 661, 661001, Short, H26/24RO, 13/2/29
MT 2114 was the first of the AEC Regent 661 types to be built and was extensively demonstrated around the country. It was demonstrated to BCT in 1929. It had an AEC A145 7.4-litre petrol engine and an open-staircase Short Brothers body. It was sold to Halifax Corporation as their fleet number 57 in February 1930.

99 (OF 3959)
Opposite: The Leyland Titan TD1 99 (OF 3959) had a lowbridge fifty-one-seat Leyland body and was one of the first TD1s to have an enclosed staircase – they had only been available since the summer of 1929. It was the last new vehicle to be purchased in this elaborated gold-lined livery. The Inner Circle was being operated by the thirty-five lowbridge Short-bodied AEC 507 Pickpocket Specials and it is possible that 99 was eventually purchased to eradicate this illegal thieving; however, the ADC 507s were all redundant by June 1934 and 99 went just eight months later, as the newly introduced Daimler COG5 chassis were able to get under the Inner Circle's two bridges without resorting to a lowbridge layout. (BCT)

MT 2114

Above: The prototype AEC Regent MT 2114 was demonstrated to the Transport Department and is posed in front of typical 1920s detached houses in suburban Birmingham. The front offside view shows off the large, comfortable enclosed driver's cab and its demonstration livery of off-white with three red bands. It stayed on loan from 4 to 18 March 1929, running a total of 2,091 miles in service on the Inner Circle 8 route. The Short Brothers outside-staircase body looked like a lowbridge bus from the ground, but in fact had a 'camel-roof' hump running above the central upper saloon gangway. (BCT)

MT 2114

Below: The rear of the bus shows the outside staircase arrangement of this six-bay Short body has a more substantial arrangement that on other contemporary bus bodies. Even the open staircase looks reasonably safe! On the credit side the actual platform is commodious with even the conductor being able to get a modicum of protection. The demonstration of this bus instantly made everything that had gone before obsolete and led to BCT purchasing 168 AEC Regents with piano-front-style bodies built by Brush, English Electric, Metro-Cammell, Short and Vulcan. The irony was that no BCT-purchased AEC Regent ever had an outside staircase. (BCT)

97 (UK 8047)

By the end of 1929, a Guy Invincible FC chassis with a five-bay Hall Lewis forty-eight-seater body and an enclosed staircase was placed on long-term loan to Birmingham for a demonstration period of four years. The 97 (UK 8047) replacement Gardner 6LW engine greatly improved the economy of the bus, but the high-framed chassis with a two-step rear entrance did not make the bus viable for use in the city. It is posing in Gosta Green with the Nechells trolleybus wires above the rear of the double-decker. (Guy Motors)

97 (UK 8047), Guy Invincible FC, FC23497, Hall Lewis, H24/24R, 12/1929
UK 8047 was demonstrated to BCT by Guy Motors of Wolverhampton from December 1929 to December 1933. It was originally fitted with a Guy 7.672-litre petrol engine, but this was replaced in 1932 with a Gardner 6LW 8.4-litre diesel engine. The high bonnet line and broad radiator rather spoilt the bus's appearance. UK 8047 was returned to Guys in January 1934.

96 (UK 8911), Guy FCX66, FCX 23547, Hall Lewis, H24/24R, 4/6/1930
From 1928, BCT were looking for a large double-deck bus chassis that could cope with heavily loaded new bus services expanding into the new council-built suburbs. UK 8911 was a six-wheeled FCX66 model and was demonstrated by Guy Motors Ltd, Wolverhampton, from 14 June 1930 to 11 January 1932. It had a Guy 7.672-litre petrol engine and a Guy six-bay H27/26R body with an exaggerated style of piano-front body and enclosed staircase that was very similar in style to the bodies on the two Guy-bodied BTX demonstrator trolleybuses UK 8341 and OG 9886. UK 8911 was broken up by Guys in November 1937.

96 (UK 8911)

This Guy FCX66 was operated from Harborne Garage where all the six-wheeled demonstrators were housed. The Guy FCX66 was a rear bogied version of the Invincible model with an 18-foot 6-inch wheelbase and length of nearly 30 feet. The somewhat antiquated Guy body design had an exaggerated style of 'piano front' between the cab and the front of the set-back upper saloon, but seating only fifty-three. Although 96 (UK 8911) remained in the city for nineteen months, running on the Outer Circle route, it did not generate any orders. (Guy Motors)

98 (WM 5621), *Vulcan Emperor VWBD, VWBD5, Brush, H27/21R, 10/1930*

WM 5621 was a Vulcan Motors Limited, Southport, Emperor demonstrated between 4 October1930 and 8 January 1931. It was fitted with a Vulcan Monarch six-cylinder petrol engine. It was later used by several operators cut down to a thirty-seater single-decker and was withdrawn after just two month's service by Crosville in September 1934.

98 (VM 5621)

Overleaf above: This is probably the vehicle demonstrated to Birmingham for two months at the end of 1930, although it was painted in full BCT livery. This was the fifth Vulcan Emperor VWBD to be built and was the second demonstrator. The body was built by Brush to an uncomfortable-looking design. Ironically, Vulcan supplied thirty-five very attractive bodies to Birmingham's standard piano-front design between August and November 1930. VM 5621 was offered to Glasgow Corporation in December 1931, which had bought twenty-five air-braked Cowieson-bodied Emperors, but the offer was politely declined. VM 5621 is parked near to Lord Street in Southport where Vulcan had their factory. (D. R. Harvey Collection)

94 (VR 9019), Crossley Condor, 90429, Crossley, L26/24R, –/1930
94 (VR 9019) was a Crossley Motors Limited, Stockport, and was on hire to
Birmingham from 10 October 1930 to December 1931. It had a Crossley 6.8-litre
petrol engine. The chassis was dismantled in 1936. No known photograph.

96 (RG 1675), Crossley Condor, 90475, Crossley, H24/24R, 10/1930
96 was a demonstrator from Crossley Motors, Manchester, for one month only
from 21 June 1932 to July 1932. It was exhibited at the 1930 Commercial Motor
Show and was fitted with a Crossley 38/110 6.796-litre petrol engine. It was tried by
Aberdeen Corporation from November 1930 to March 1931. RG 1675 was fitted
with 'Crossley Patent Effortless Gearchange' gearbox in May 1931 which replaced its
original four-speed sliding mesh gearbox. 96 and 97 stayed in Birmingham for only
three weeks in order to compare their different transmissions. RG 1675 was broken up
by Crossley Motors in 1936. No known photograph.

97 (RG 1676), Crossley Condor, 90476, Crossley, H24/24R, 11/1930
97 was the second Crossley Condor on loan as a demonstrator from Crossley Motors,
for one month from 21 June 1932. Fitted with a Crossley 38/110 6.796-litre petrol
engine it was originally registered by Aberdeen Corporation and demonstrated to BCT
from November 1930 to March 1931. Both 96 and 97 had standard Crossley six-bay
bodies with the roofline raised over the upper saloon gangway, which was Crossley's
version of the Short's camel-roof design. RG 1676 received Crossley 9.12-litre Crossley
diesel engine and an 'autochange' gearbox in July 1931. In 1932 it was demonstrated to
Nottingham City Transport and then to Northampton Corporation, who purchased it as
their 66 in December 1933. It was rebodied by East Lancs H30/24R in March 1944 and
was destroyed in the Edge Lane tram depot fire in June 1947 while on loan to Liverpool.

97 (RG 1676)

Previous page: 97 (RG 1676), the second of the Crossley demonstrator 'twins', was original fitted with a normal crash gearbox, and after its time in Birmingham it went back to Crossley Motors where it was fitted with the Crossley VR6 9.12-litre high-revving direct-injection oil engine with an Autovac mounted on the lower saloon bulkhead. In this form it was demonstrated to Nottingham Corporation in 1932, where it was photographed on hire to that Corporation. (D. R. Harvey Collection)

95 (UK 7456), Sunbeam Sikh K101, 10123, Dodson, H35/32R, 7/1929

Sunbeam Sikh K101 six-wheeled double-decker UK 7456 was demonstrated to BCT by the Sunbeam Motor Company of Wolverhampton from 5 November 1930 to 1 December 1930. Only three Sikh chassis were ever constructed and one of them was rebuilt as a trolleybus, becoming the prototype Sunbeam MS1 chassis and bought by Wolverhampon Corporation as their 95 (JW 526). Unfortunately, the Sikh chassis was Sunbeam's last throw of the dice before the company was forced into receivership and taken over by the Rootes Group. It eventually became Derby Corporation's 44 in May 1933 and was scrapped by them in 1940.

95 (UK 7456)

Above: The six-bay Dodson sixty-seven-seater body on the Sikh chassis looks impressive as UK 7456 climbs from Darlington Street into Queen Square, Wolverhampton, sometime during 1932 when 95 (UK 7456) is seen in service. It is following an archaic-looking Guy BTX trolleybus and in comparison the bus looks quite up to date, but lurking underneath was Sunbeam's own unreliable 7.982-litre engine, a very troublesome rear bogie and transmission and brakes that were dire. Even Wolverhampton, its home town, failed to be impressed and it was returned to the Marston Road factory of Sunbeams. During its period of three weeks demonstrating in Birmingham the Sikh clocked up exactly 4,200 miles in service. Most of the buildings on the right in Queen Square still remain. The equestrian bronze statue of Prince Albert (1819–61) was the first in the country to be erected by public subscription and is known locally as 'the man on the 'oss'. It was unveiled by Queen Victoria in November 1866 – her first public engagement after Albert's death five years earlier. (D. R. Harvey Collection)

3

The Development of Modern Pre-war Single-deckers: 1929–36

The First Single-Deckers

The first modern-looking single-deckers were thirty normal-control Guy Conquest Cs with Guy B26F bodies that entered service in 1929 and 1930. This number of single-deckers would remain around the same for the requirements of BCT until the mid-1960s. Though neither the first BCT single-deckers nor demonstrators, these buses did open up numerous interurban services and routes beyond tram termini.

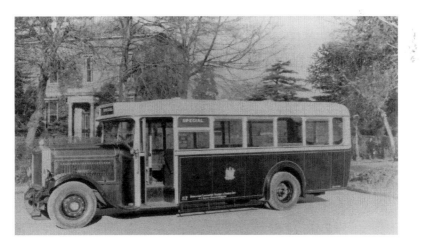

57 (OF 3966)
The Guy Conquest C was an imposing yet attractive-looking bus in its normal-control condition, although with its long bonnet it seemed to be more engine than bus. 57 (OF 3966) was one of the ten that entered service in September 1929 and were identical to the buses numbered 61–80, dating from early 1930. Bought for one-man operation with a small-capacity Guy B25F body in order to comply with the then current regulations, within two years the Board of Trade Regulations for one-man-operation use had altered and, along with all the others, 57 was rebuilt to forward control by Guy Motors, in this case in November 1931. (G. H. F. Atkins)

76 (OF 6086)

Above: After conversion to forward control in December 1931, 76 (OF 6086) was further modified by receiving an AEC petrol engine and gearbox from one of the 1930 AEC Regent 661s during 1934. The conversion certainly made the bus more useful with a B32F layout, but it hardly improved its appearance. After withdrawal in January 1936, 76 was placed into the ancillary fleet as a driver trainer and renumbered 50. It was finally withdrawn in the spring of 1945. (D. R. Harvey Collection)

86 (OV 4086)

Below: On a miserable day in November 1931, a brand-new Morris-Commercial Dictator posed for its official BCT photograph. Their MCCW B34F bodies were among the earliest metal-framed single-deckers to be built. Weighing 5 tons 12 cwt, 86 (OV 4086) had a somewhat austere-looking body, which was of a much better quality when compared to the somewhat frail Morris-Commercial 7.698-litre petrol engine. There were fourteen of these single-deckers that were built to augment the rebuilt Guy Conquest C. 86 was withdrawn on 31 August 1945. (BCT)

44 (AOP 44)
Above: In order to replace the aging six-year-old Guy Conquest Cs, twenty Metro-Cammell Daimler COG5s were purchased and numbered 42–61. 44 (AOP 44) was used for the official BCT photograph and entered service on 22 May 1935. The body style was an updated and curvaceous structure based on the bodies built on the 1933 Morris Commercial Dictators. During the Second World War, 44 was used as an ambulance fitted with rows of stretchers from 24 August 1934 until 31 December 1945. It was used in this capacity to take wounded military personnel from various railway stations to Selly Oak Hospital. 44 reverted to a bus and it was withdrawn on 31 July 1950. (BCT)

62 (AOP 62)
Below: Fifteen further Daimler COG5s with Strachan B34F bodywork were supplied by the Acton-based coachbuilders that were similar to the contemporary MCCW bodies being delivered between August and October 1935. The Strachan bodies differed from the MCCW single-deckers by having a slightly more angled windscreen, guttering over the porch entrance and slightly more flaired lower saloon panels. These buses were thrashed in the Second World War with perimeter seating and extra space for another twenty standee passengers. 62 was withdrawn on 30 June 1950. (G.Burrows)

4

AEC Regents: 1929–31

339 (OF 3971), AEC Regent, 661, 661011, Brush H26/24R, 1/1930
Before any of the new range of AEC Regent 661s were demonstrated or bought, Birmingham had pre-production prototypes with chassis numbers 661010 and 011 delivered in October and early November 1929 with Brush totally enclosed bodywork. Over the next two years, piano-front-bodied petrol-engined Regents became the standard BCT bus.

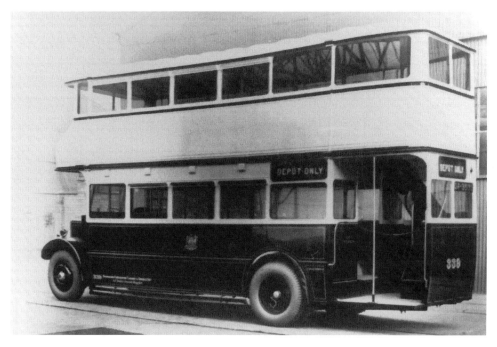

339 (OF 3971)
This was the granddaddy of the standard Birmingham bus. 339 (OF 3971) was the eleventh prototype AEC Regent 661 chassis and was distinguishable from its twin 338 by having a curved badge surround on the top of the radiator. 339 had a Brush H26/24R body, which set the design of BCT bodywork from 1929 until 1954. It entered service on 6 November 1929, though not for long. It was withdrawn on 1 June 1930 and returned to AEC who replaced the chassis, which had a number of non-standard features and a similar Brush body that had a H27/21R layout. This is the original 339 that is parked outside the Brush factory in November 1929. (Brush)

357 (OF 3989)

At 12.55 p.m. on a warm sunny day in August 1930, four AEC Regent 661s stand in Paradise Street. Such a day would be ideal for going to the races and in those days Birmingham had a racecourse at Bromford Bridge, which survived until its last meeting on 21 June 1965. Behind the bus is the Birmingham & Midland Institute designed by Edward Barry and opened in 1860 and which pioneered adult education classes in Britain. The leading bus is Brush-bodied 357 (OF 3989), filling up with racegoers. Two of the same class stand behind it, but the second and third are two brand-new English Electric-bodied AEC Regents from the 369–408 batch. (G. H. F. Atkins)

96 (OF 8368), AEC Regent 661, 661035, Short, H28/24R, 1/1930

OF 8368 was an AEC Regent 661 demonstrator for Short Brothers Ltd and was trialled from January 1930 until March 1930. The metal-framed body used aluminium alloys for the upper saloon floor, frame and roof and had a body design similar to the Short-bodied BCT lightweight tram 842. 96 was purchased by Birmingham Corporation Transport in March 1930 and was renumbered 368 soon afterwards. It remained largely unaltered during its life and because of the extra quality of its ornate interior, the window pan design and the raised waist rails it was known as the 'Showboat'. It was finally taken out of service on 31 July 1944.

96 (OF 8368)

Above: The Short Brothers body on 96 AEC Regent 661 was a one-off design with a piano-front that sloped more than other of BCT's AEC Regent 661s delivered between 1929 and 1932. The bus still has the rather splendid large front sidelights as well as its primrose-painted bonnet top. Renumbered 368 (OF 8368), it stands at the bus stop in Paradise Street in around 1932, working on the 1A service to Moseley and Acocks Green. To the left is Ratcliff Place and the Town Hall, while in the distant corner of Victoria Square and New Street is Galloway's Corner. (R. Marshall)

368 (OF 8368)

Below: Picking up passengers in Colmore Row on 8 May 1937 is 368 (OF 8368) during the celebrations for the coronation of George VI and Queen Elizabeth. The bus is easily recognisable by its deep piano front, the low-mounted destination box and the positioning of the middle blue livery band. The unusually designed rear end featured three upper saloon windows, as found on the ends of tram 842. OF 8368 had a curved staircase, making it almost certainly the last Birmingham bus not to have a straight one. The AEC Regent 661 is working on the cross-city 34 service to Quinton. (D. R. Harvey Collection)

JF 223, AEC Regent, 661129, Ransomes, Sims & Jefferies, H27/22R, –/1930

JF 223 was an AEC Motors Limited demonstrator built for City of Leicester Tramways in July 1930 and was fitted with the new AEC 7.4-litre petrol engine. It passed to E. W. Campion, Nottingham, by August 1932 and then to Barton, Chilwell, 248 in November 1935. The London General-style ST body had an enclosed straight staircase and a seating capacity of only forty-nine.

JF 223

Demonstrator JF 223 is standing at the AEC factory grounds in Southall with members of the AEC management and representatives from Leicester. JF 223 had an LGOC-style Ransomes Simms & Jefferies forty-nine-seat body and came to Birmingham in July 1930. It had a new type of 110-hp 7.4-litre petrol engine for Birmingham's engineers to test, but the bus wasn't a great success either in Birmingham or Leicester. (D. R. Harvey Collection)

More Production Regents with Different Manufacturers Bodies

374 (OG374)

Overleaf above: The English Electric-bodied AEC Regent 661s, of which 374 (OG374) was one of the forty forty-eight-seaters delivered in the second half of 1930, were the first in the fleet to have corresponding fleet and registration numbers. It stands in Perry Barr Garage's entrance road leading onto Wellhead Lane. Although BCT purchased 168 AEC Regent 661 chassis, the bodies were supplied by five bodybuilders: Brush, English Electric, Vulcan, Short and Metro-Cammell. They were built to the same overall design with subtle differences, but all with fully enclosed driver's cabs and staircases and with a front axle weight reducing piano-front arrangement. (D. R. Harvey Collection)

392 (OG 392)

Above: All twenty-four BCT buses converted to the producer gas system operated on the extremely hilly Kingstanding service, which meant that they laboured up the steep gradients to north of the River Tame Valley. Waiting at the Finchley Road/Kings Road terminus of the 33 route on Saturday 31 July 1943 is 392 (OG 392), an English Electric-bodied AEC Regent 661 that used a producer gas trailer from June 1943 until June 1944 and then was immediately withdrawn without ever being converted to run on petrol again. Kingstanding was an exposed heathland part of Perry Barr UDC until 1928, but by 1932 Birmingham Council had built over 6,300 houses on the land for around 30,000 people. The last new BCT tram route extension had been opened to Stechford on Tuesday 26 August 1928, so it was perhaps surprising that motorbuses were preferred on the 33 route introduced on 18 August 1930 to Ellerton Road, which was extended to its second terminus at Finchley Road in January 1933. (L. W. Perkins)

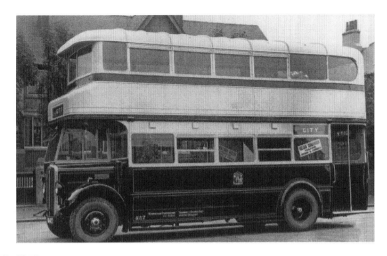

427 (OG 427)

Above: Awaiting delivery from the bodybuilding works in Southport during September 1930 is 427 (OG 427), one of the thirty-four AEC Regent 661s bodied by Vulcan. These buses were some of the few 'modern' double-deck bodies built by Vulcan, but would have benefitted by not having the piano front between the decks. They were also the last double-deckers delivered to BCT that did not comply with the 1930 Road Traffic Act with regard to the statutory number of emergency exits, as there was no cut out at nearside rear of the platform and no emergency exit window in the rear dome. 427 was not a long-lived bus as it was withdrawn on 30 July 1937. (Vulcan)

451 (OV 4451)

Below: Of all the British municipalities only Birmingham and Bradford extensively rebodied pre-war vehicles during the Second World War with new utility bodywork, this only applying to the latter's trolleybus fleet. A paper sticker in the front window shows that 451 (OV 4451), dating from August 1931 and formerly fitted with a Short body, will shortly be on its way 'DIRECT TO VILLA PARK', with a stipulation that it unloads in Witton Lane. 451 was one of fifty petrol-engined AEC Regent 661s built between 1929 and 1931 to be rebodied with Brush MOS bodies, in this case in August 1943, and had a straight staircase taken from one of the original bodies, reducing the seating capacity to a H30/21R layout. In 1948 it is waiting on the wrong side of Carrs Lane for a rush of Villa Park-bound fans outside Carr Lane Congregational Chapel, built in 1820 and rebuilt in 1876 by Yeoville Thomason, who designed Birmingham Council House. (S. N. J. White)

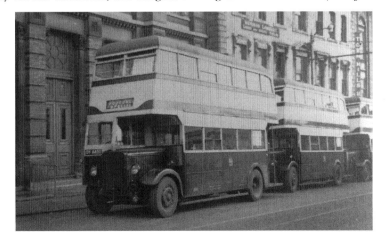

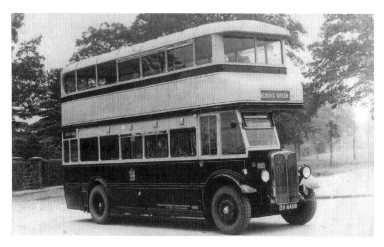

468 (OV 4468)

The last large order of Short composite construction bodies supplied to BCT was perhaps the most attractive of all the BCT piano-front bodies. Numbered 444–483, 468 (OV 4468), an AEC Regent 661, entered service on 11 September 1931 and was withdrawn on New Year's Eve 1944. It is parked in the service road in Olton Boulevard East when brand new. It led a fairly undistinguished life, except being one of the thirty vehicles that spent three weeks in London during the height of the Blitz – 30 October 1940 until 23 November 1940. Ironically, they were all returned early to Birmingham because of the extensive wartime destruction at Hockley Garage. (BCT)

209 (OG 209), AEC Regent 661, 661766, MCCW, H27/21R, 11/11/1930

209 (OG 209) was an AEC Regent 661 and was the first vehicle to ever receive a MCCW all-metal body. It was converted to operate on producer gas, pulling a coke-filled trailer during 1944 on the 33 route to Kingstanding and was a rare case of one of these buses to be reconverted to petrol at an unknown date. It was withdrawn on 19 September 1945.

209 (OG 209)

When new, 209 (OG 209) suffered the indignity of having a railway wagon shunted into its side to show off the structural integrity of the still new metal-framed body concept. A Metropolitan-Cammell advertisement published in a trade journal on 15 April 1932 shows the neat lines of the body, whose square-cornered saloon windows reveal that the body is metal framed. The inset on the advertisement shows the structure of the bodywork. The bus had a BCT type straight staircase. (Electric Railway, Bus and Tram Journal)

209 (OG 209)

Above: Towards the end of its service life, 209 (OG 209) was moved to Yardley Wood Garage. Looking a little battered, 209 stands at the garage in Yardley Wood Road on Thursday 12 July 1945 as an inspector poses with the regular crew before they go into Birmingham on a 24 route shortworking to Ethel Street. (L. W. Perkins)

492 (OV 4492)

Below: The final of the AEC Regent 661s were twenty metal-framed bodies by Metro-Cammell, which were their contract five. These were the first batch of metal-framed bodies built by the company and were based on the prototype body fitted to 209 (OG 209). These bodies could be distinguished by having square-cornered saloon windows. 492 (OV 4492) entered service on 1 January 1932 and was on loan to London Passenger Transport Board from 30 October 1940 to 23 November 1940. It was posed for a BCT official photograph in Harborne Lane when new. 486 survived as a caravan for many years and is now beautifully restored at the Wythall Bus Museum. (BCT)

5

The Search for Something Modern: 1931–35

93 (PL 3078), Dennis Lance, 125004, ?, H27/24R, –/1931

This vehicle was a Dennis Bros, Guildford, demonstrator and was on hire from 7 March 1931 to 15 May 1931 and had a Dennis 6.13-litre petrol engine. Not much is known about the V-fronted body's origins, although it could have been built by Park Royal. Dennis must have had high hopes of obtaining a BCT order as neighbouring Walsall was at this time exclusively purchasing Dennis chassis. PL 3078 was eventually operated by East Kent Road Car, Canterbury, from 1935 until 1937.

93 (PL 3078)

PL 3078 was only the fourth Dennis Lance to be constructed and was tried out on the Inner Circle 8 route, running 3,423 miles in March 1931 in a near all-over blue livery with three cream bands. It appears to be posed outside Barford Street Garage in front of the grim three-storey Victorian back-to-back courtyards opposite the bus garage. Barford Street was the first operational purpose-built garage to be used by the Transport Department, having previously been a factory and opened in June 1925. (D. R. Harvey Collection)

92 (MV 489), AEC Renown, 663952, Brush, H33/25R, 10/1931
92 (MV 489) was an impressive-looking six-wheel bus that was on loan to BCT as an AEC demonstrator from 23 October 1931 to December 1932 when it was purchased. It was one of only three of the short wheelbase Renown 663s built other than for London General. This vehicle was fitted with an AEC A145 7.4-litre petrol engine and was purchased by BCT in December 1932. It was only in service as a bus until January 1938 when it was converted into Service Vehicle 15 in February 1938 as a mobile crane and breakdown lorry with equipment taken from OP 238. It was always garaged at Miller Street, where it was given the nickname 'The Ambulance'.

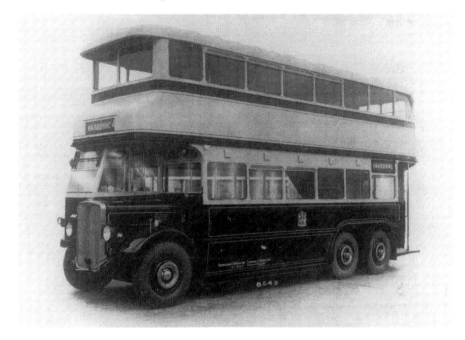

92 (MV 489)
Above: The massive 92 (MV 489) was photographed by Brush's official photographer in October 1931, who has unfortunately airbrushed out any indication as to where the picture was taken. Regrettably, this is the only known picture of 92, taken during its four-year operational life as a bus. As the destination blind suggests, it was operated from Harborne Garage and amassed some 178,605 miles trundling around the Outer Circle route. So how did it manage to miss so many photographers' lenses? (D. R. Harvey Collection)

92 (MV 489)
Overleaf above: The solitary AEC Renown 663 had a very short life as bus 92. In February 1938 it received the crane from Service Vehicle 15 (the former Karrier DD6 bus OP 238) and was given the same number in the auxiliary fleet, becoming the Transport Department's main recovery vehicle. MV 489 is standing alongside the soon-to-be abandoned tram tracks in High Street outside the Oxford Restaurant, who sold the best meat and potato pies in Birmingham. It is being used as a standby shunter, with a large wooden beam to push the trams that were coasted down Carrs Lane as they travelled across the city on the evenings of 3 and 4 July 1953 on their way for eventual scrapping at Kyotts Lake Road Works. Of the sixty trams that were moved on those two evenings only one needed a shove by 'The Ambulance'. MV 489 was withdrawn in September 1961. (J. C. Gillham)

95 (KJ 2918), Tilling-Stevens E60A6, 9103 Short, H28/21R, –/1931

This vehicle was on loan from Tilling-Stevens, Maidstone. It had a Tilling-Stevens petrol engine and had a Short body built to the then current Birmingham piano-front style of body. It was on loan from 11 December 1931 to 30 January 1933 and was returned to TSM.

95 (KJ 2918)

Given the fleet number 95 in the demonstration fleet number series, KJ 2918 was registered by TSM Motors of Maidstone with Kent CC in December 1931. It was bodied by Short Brothers, who were based nearby in Rochester and were supplying piano-front bodies of this style to Birmingham. The body had a very deep windscreen due to the low-mounted bonnet line of the TSM E60A6 chassis. 95 was used on the Inner Circle 8 service from Barford Street Garage. Despite being worked very hard, it was apparently very reliable and accrued some 32,976 miles in its thirteen-month loan period. (TSM Motors)

442 (OJ 5442)
Not quite what it seems! This is what 442 would have looked like as this bus travels along College Road on the 7 route on 14 September 1933. The Crossley Condor 442 (OJ 5442) received an almost new Vulcan H27/21R body from an AEC Regent on arrival in December 1932. These Southport-built bodies were characterised by the large single-pane upper saloon emergency window as well as the usual BCT straight staircase. (D. R. Harvey Collection)

442 (OJ 5442), Crossley Condor, 91057, Vulcan, H27/21R, –/1932
442 (OJ 5442) had a Crossley VR6 9.12-litre diesel engine and was on extended loan from 2 December 1932 until 10 December 1937. The Vulcan H27/21R body was from AEC Regent 661 442, OG 442, which had been prematurely withdrawn in December 1932. It was sold to Cashmore (dealer), Great Bridge, in September 1938 and was broken up.

93 (AHX 63), AEC Q 761, 761001, MCCW, H33/29F, 10/1932
AHX 63 was the first of twenty-three AEC Q 761 double-deckers to be constructed and had an offside, mounted A169 7.4-litre petrol engine located outside the chassis frame between the front and rear axles. It was on loan from AEC Ltd, Southall, as a demonstrator between 28 January 1933 and 30 January 1934 as H31/29F and was painted in a mainly dark blue livery with three off-white livery bands for its demonstration period. Not long after being fitted with an oil engine and subsequently purchased on 16 November 1935, the bus was repainted in the normal fleet colours. 93 was withdrawn on 23 October 1940.

93 (AHX 63)

93 (AHX 63) stands in the grounds of AEC's Southall factory grounds in its original livery in October 1932 with its original AEC petrol engine in situ. It ran in this original condition with the predominantly dark blue livery until it was converted to a diesel oil engine in 1935. (AEC)

93 (AHX 63)

About to turn into Corporation Street after having travelled down New Street from the distant Town Hall in Victoria Square is 93 (AHX 63). The date is 1936 and having been finally purchased by BCT in the previous October, is now repainted in the full Birmingham livery of dark blue and cream with two blue bands on the predominantly cream upper part of the body. The bus is working from Harborne Garage on the 3 route from Queen's Park, Harborne. AHX 63 was the only petrol-engined AEC Q to be converted to oil and had recently been down seated to a H29/27F layout. Despite being a very advanced design with its offside mounted engine and front entrance, 93 covered some 110,216 miles in its nearly nine years operating in Birmingham. (D. R. Harvey Collection)

94 (TF 7310), Leyland TD2c, 130, Leyland, L24/24R, 5/1932

This Leyland Titan TD2c was on extended loan from Leyland Motors, Leyland, Lancashire, between 16 February 1933 and 31 May 1934. It had a Leyland 7.6-litre petrol engine coupled to a Lysholm-Smith torque converter gearbox. This had a variable torque converter, which took the bus up to around 20 mph. The torque selector, looking like a normal gear lever, was located where the second gear would have been on a conventional H-configured gearbox. Pull the gear selector straight back and there was the direct top gear, which took the bus up to its maximum speed. There was also, of course, a reverse gear.

94 (TF 7310)

When the demonstration period for 94 (TF 7310) ended at the end of May 1934, the lowbridge Leyland Titan TD2c was returned to Leyland. Immediately after this happened the bus was posed with over forty of the Leyland workforce, who appear to be queuing to get on the bus. 94 was painted in a heavily gold-lined livery used until around 1930. It still has its BCT 94 fleet number on the rear panel and, except for seeming to be a somewhat dusty appearance, it seems to be in good order after over fourteen months' work in Birmingham. This demonstration eventually led to the purchase of 964–968 (COX 964–968). Leyland Motors sold TF 7310 to J. James of Ammanford as their 145. (D. R. Harvey Collection)

91 (OV 4848)

OV 4848 was the first Morris-Commercial Imperial one to be built and was on long-term loan from 19 January 1932 to June 1936. It had a Morris-Commercial 7.698-litre petrol engine and a Short body very similar to 95, KJ 2912, but with only a vestige of a piano front. Morris Motors were trying to break into the heavyweight double- and single-deck bus market and BCT saw their opportunity to obtain new buses and support Birmingham-based industry during the Depression. Initial promise, however, soon became a long list of chassis and engine problems with the Imperials and soon this led to a request for Morris to provide the chassis with Gardner oil engines. After this was refused future orders went to Daimler.

91 (OV 4848)

OV 4848 is almost new when posed alongside the River Medway in Rochester, Kent, in December 1931 immediately after it had appeared on the bodybuilder's sales stand at the 1931 Olympia Commercial Motor Show. The lightweight body is painted in BCT's blue and cream livery. During its four-year stay in Birmingham, it was allocated to Perry Barr Garage. The demonstration period with the Corporation was sufficiently successful that a further fifty Imperials – out of a total production run of eighty-three – were operated by Birmingham. (Short Brothers)

6

Speculative Demonstrators and Orders to BCT Specification: 1931–33

As a result of the successful demonstration of OV 4848 in 1932 and the wish to support local industry the next three buses were Morris-Commercial Imperial HDs. Although not actually demonstrators, they were fitted by three different coachbuilders, specifically Brush, English Electric and Gloucester R.C.W, as speculative ventures in an attempt to get a large body contract from BCT.

504 (OC 504) Morris Commercial Imperial HD, 082, Brush, H29/22R, 19/2/1934
504 (OC 504) was a Morris Commercial Imperial HD fitted with a somewhat frail Morris Commercial 7.698-ohv petrol engine. 504 (OC 504) was the first of the trio to enter service on 19 February 1934, though this was two months after the last of the forty-seven Metro-Cammell-bodied Imperials entered service. It was withdrawn on 30 April 1942 and was sold for scrap in October 1946.

504 (OC 504)

Previous page: The attractive Brush body on 504 (OC 504) had a trace of the earlier BCT piano-front styling and it was the last bus to have the windows set deeply into the framework. Brush put a lot of effort into this metal-framed bus body in the attempt to gain a substantial order from Birmingham and it was delivered in an exhibition-quality finish, with even the surrounds to the front destination box being chromed. The bus was operated from Perry Barr Garage and would become the longest lived of the three odd-bodied Imperials. (L. W. Perkins)

505 (OC 505), Morris Commercial 'Imperial' HD, 080, English Electric, H25/22R, 1/3/1934

505 (OC 505) was another petrol-engined Morris Commercial Imperial. It had an English Electric composite-framed body and entered service on 1 March 1934. When new the body on 505 only had a seating capacity for forty-seven passengers. It was stored after withdrawal on 14 March 1941 and was sold to Devey, Shenstone.

505 (OC 505)

Above: The bus waiting in the West Works of the English Electric Company factory in Preston prior to delivery to Birmingham is OC 505. English Electric appears to have dusted down the BCT body drawings for the piano-front AEC Regents 369–408 of 1930 and put an almost straight raking front on the body. The composite construction bodywork is a steel and ash framework. 505 is equipped with four sets of Perry Barr Garage's destination blinds, where it spent its entire career in Birmingham until it was taken out of service on 14 February 1941 due to the chronic shortage of engine spare parts. It stood in store until sold for scrap in October 1946. (English Electric)

506 (OC 506), Morris Commercial Imperial HD, 081, Gloucester RCW, H26/22R, 9/5/1934

506 (OC 506) was the third odd-bodied Morris Commercial Imperial. It had a good-looking, if extremely rare, Gloucester RCW-built, forty-eight-seat body and was one of only a handful of double-decker chassis bodied by the GRCW. Surprisingly, in view of the excellent reputation of the company's railway carriages and wagons, its bus bodies were not very durable.

506 (OC 506)

506 (OC 506) pulls away from the Beauchamp Avenue bus stop halfway down the steep Hamstead Hill on 13 August 1938. The Perry Barr Garage-based Morris-Commercial is working on the cross-city 16A route, which was extended from Friary Road to Beauchamp Avenue on 27 October 1937. It will reverse into Beauchamp Avenue before returning across the city to Church Road, Yardley, as a 15. Although seemingly in good condition, it would be taken out of service at the end of the following June and sold to Deveys for scrap in October 1946. This gives this bus the unenviable record of spending more than half of its twelve-year life in storage. What a waste! (R. T. Coxon)

Production Imperials

The production Morris-Commercial Imperials with MCCW bodywork were not a great success as the chassis was too lightweight, the 7.698-litre petrol engine tended to backfire and require constant tuning and had a very short crankshaft life, which all contributed to making them very thirsty, expensive to repair and prone to breakdowns. The gearboxes on the Imperials were also awkward to handle, they gave a very rough and bouncy ride and had a very short brake pad life expectancy.

530 (OC 530)

Despite purchasing three Morris-Commercial Imperial double-deckers and having another one on a long-term loan, each with a non-standard body, BCT purchased another forty-seven of these locally built chassis fitted with an earl type of the very successful metal-framed Metro-Cammell H28/22R bodywork between September and November 1933. In 1935 the Barrows Lane terminus of the 15A service was within hailing distance of the double-bay-windowed Ring o' Bells public house and only half a mile from the Outer Circle route at the Yew Tree Public house on Stoney Lane. 530 (OC 530), barely two years old and with its seating capacity recently increased to fifty-four, stands in the tree-lined road waiting for the conductor to change the destination blind to show 'Handsworth Wood 16' for the return journey. This Yardley terminus was as close as Corporation buses ever got to the old village centre and its thirteenth-century church. (F. Lloyd)

I'm Just a Solitary Guy

208 (OC 8208), Guy Arab, FD23971, MCCW, H29/22R, 4/5/1934
208 was purchased to trial the Gardner 6LW 8.4-litre diesel engine. It was MCCW body contract 41 and looked very similar to those fitted to Morris-Commercial Imperials 507–553. Bus 208 was the last in the fleet to have a two-letter registration mark. The Metro-Cammell bodywork was to the BCT interim design, also found on the Morris-Commercial Imperials and the fifty-six-wheeled Leyland TTBD2 trolleybuses. It was perhaps surprising that no further pre-war Guy Arab buses were bought as the Gardner 5LW Daimler COG5 reigned supreme in the city's bus fleet. 208 was reseated H30/24R during 1935 and withdrawn on 28 February 1945.

208 (OC 8208)
Aston Villa's latest football match has just finished, and all around the traffic island in Witton Square in 1935 are a number of Football Special buses, including, outside the Co-Op, an ADC 507 with an outside staircase Short Brothers body. On the right, coming out of Witton Road, are two very different AECs: an outside staircase 507 model and 494 (OV 4494), an MCCW-bodied Regent built in 1931. In the foreground, on an Outer Circle shortworking to Harborne, is 208 (OC 8208), which looks as if it has just escaped the approaching swarm of fans, much to the relief of the crew. Looking like one of the MCCW-bodied Imperials, this wide-radiatored double-decker was Birmingham's solitary pre-war Guy Arab FD. (D. R. Harvey Collection)

7

Enter the Daimler COG5

100 (VC 7519), Daimler CH6, 9030, Buckingham, H26/24R, 2/1931
VC 7516 was demonstrated by Daimler between 6 March 1931 and 30 June 1934. It had a Daimler 5.6-litre petrol engine and had the only 'modern' double-deck body built by John Buckingham's Coachworks in Bradford Street, Birmingham, before they fell into receivership in 1931. VC 7519 was subsequently demonstrated to Walsall Corporation, registered DH 8638, in March 1931 and it was subsequently on hire to Coventry City Transport (100) from March 1935 until the body was burnt out in 1938.

100 (VC 7519)
One of the more elusive Daimler buses became Coventry's 100 (VC 7519). This was 5.6-litre petrol-engined Daimler CH6 and was completed in February 1931. It was fitted with a H26/24R body built by Buckingham. 100 is in High Street at the stop used by the service to Coundon. (Commercial Postcard)

100 (VC 7519)
The chassis of VC 7519 was salvaged and sold to L. T. March (dealer), who had it fitted with a Walsall-built Holbrook FC–F body as DH 8638 and was sold to Dorothy Holbrook's Harmony Hussars's light entertainment orchestra, who used it until the late 1940s for both accommodation and as an instrument carrier to travel between engagements. (Advertisement for Dorothy Holbrook's Ladies Harmony Hussars)

KV 1396, Daimler COG5, 9064, Brush, H28/26R, 7/1932

KV 1396 was on loan for one month from Daimler Motor Company, Coventry, between 7 November 1933 and 15 December1933. It was the first COG5 chassis to be constructed and had for the first time the combination of a Gardner 5LW 7.0-litre engine coupled to a Wilson preselector gearbox and fluid flywheel. It was sold to Westcliffe-on-Sea, but it had proved to be economical and led the way to the future large orders by Birmingham CT for the Daimler COG5 chassis.

KV 1396

Above: If the Buckingham-bodied Daimler CH6, VC 7519 had an influence on the thinking of A. C. Baker and the Transport Committee, the demonstration of KV 1396, coming just a matter of weeks before the conversion of the Coventry Road tram route, which would use fifty state-of-the-art Leyland TTBD2 trolleybuses, made alternative ideas for future vehicles redundant overnight. Although the Brush bodywork fitted to this Daimler COG5 was to a style purchased by Leicester City Transport and not to Birmingham specifications, the combination of an oil engine and a preselector gearbox was irresistible and this bus presaged the purchase of 831 COG5s from Daimler. KV 1396 stands in the yard of the Brush body works in Loughborough when new in 1932. (Brush, Loughborough)

554 (OC 554)

Opposite above: The failure of Morris-Commercial to produce a bus with a suitable diesel engine as requested by BCT in 1934 meant that the Corporation had to look elsewhere for the next batch of buses. Suitably impressed by the Wilson preselector gearbox fitted to the CH6 demonstrator VC 7519 and KV 1396, the Daimler COG5 trialled in December 1933, an interim group of ten Daimler CP6 buses with Daimler 6.56-litre petrol engines and preselector transmission were ordered for assessment. 554 (OC 554), parked outside the BRCW works in late November 1933 prior to delivery, had H29/22R bodywork and uniquely had circular ventilation covers above the lower saloon windows. These ten were the last petrol-engine buses to be purchased by BCT. (BRCW)

Production Daimler COG5s: Improving and Developing the Breed, 1934–40

The 7.0-litre Gardner oil-engined Daimler COG5 chassis with Fluid Flywheels and Wilson preselector gearboxes were bought as a result of the demonstration of KV 1396 and became the standard bus for the Corporation. Nearly all bodied by either Metro-Cammell or Birmingham RC&W, both were manufactured in Birmingham and therefore continued the BCT policy of supporting local industry in the years after the Depression of the early 1930s. Daimler sold 794 double-decker and thirty-five single-decker COG5 chassis to Birmingham and proved to be most satisfactory, though the chassis tended to be prone to cracking.

567 (AOP 567)
Below: 567 (AOP 567), a rather gaunt-looking BRCW-bodied Daimler COG5, entered service on 18 May 1934. Three months later, on 29 August 1934, it is in Bull Street outside Edward Grey's department store when working on the 3 route to Queens Park in Harborne. These were the first BCT buses to have the Gardner 5LW 7.0-litre oil engine, fluid-flywheel and Wilson preselector gearbox combination. This produced a reliable, economical and, most importantly, easy to drive bus. The non-too-robust BRCW bodies were built in Smethwick and were among the last built without a cream moulding beneath the lower saloon windows. 567 was one of the last three of the class to be withdrawn on New Year's Eve 1948. (D.R. Harvey Collection)

569 (AOB 569)

Above: 569 (AOB 569) is parked in front of the BRCW factory just a few days prior to being delivered on 15 May 1934. This was one of the first fifteen Daimler COG5s to be purchased and had a BRCW H26/22R body that was increased to H30/24R in October 1935. BRCW products, of which BCT purchased 245 units between 1934 and 1940, followed the style of the MCCW bodies on the Imperials, but they could always be distinguished by the thicker upper saloon corner pillars and a very flat upper saloon profile, square upper saloon front windows and slightly more prominent destination boxes. The bus was fitted with a BCT-patented horizontal windscreen wiper system with two chain-driven blades held in place by the large metal frame over the windscreen. (BRCW)

588 (AOB 588)

Below: The first class of Daimler COG5s to have MCCW bodywork were numbered 579–593. Parked in Pritchatts Road at the boundary of the University of Birmingham is 588 (AOB 588), just prior to it entering service on 12 June 1934. When compared to the fully lined-out Metro-Cammell bodywork on the Morris-Commercial Dictators those on all the COG5s had thicker front upper saloon side body pillars, making for a less attractively styled body. The MCCW bodies were a neater-looking design than the BRCW examples with a rounded front destination box and less domed roof profile. (BCT)

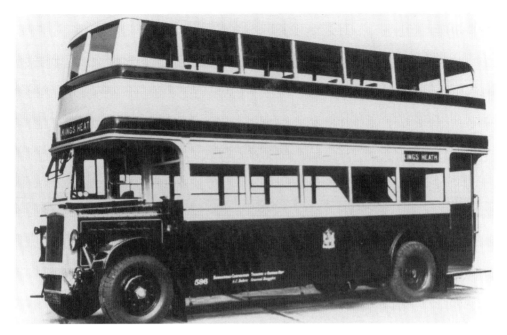

596 (AOG 596)

Above: The 594–633 class of MCCW H26/22R-bodied Daimler COG5 were the first buses in the fleet to have a cream waist rail below the lower saloon windows. This modification to the livery saw the demise of the gold lining out on the bodywork, with the only remnant being that around the bonnet top and sides. 596 (AOG 596) was exhibited in this condition at the 1934 Olympia Commercial Motor Show. The bus was reseated to H30/24R in August 1935 and remained in service until 31 January 1949. (BCT)

622 (AOG 622), etc.

Below: One of the most famous publicity photographs for Birmingham Corporation was taken at the University of Birmingham on 19 January 1935. With just four exceptions from the earlier 579–593 class of 1934 MCCW-bodied Daimler COG5s, distinguishable by their blue painted cab apron panels, all the buses are in the new livery with cream waist rails led by 622 (AOG 622) on the right, which entered service on 37 December 1934, and on the left 629 (AOG 629), delivered on 12 December 1934. (BCT)

664 (AOG 664)

Above: Working on the Sandon Road 6 route, 664 (AOG 664) entered service on 1 February 1935 and was one of the forty BRCW-bodied Daimler COG5s delivered from December 1934. It is in Victoria Square outside the Council House. It is carrying a slipboard on the radiator, which shows the same destination point shown in the route number blind. 664 was withdrawn on 30 June 1948. (G. H. F. Atkins)

682 (AOG 682)

Below: The search for alternative bodybuilders for the large orders of Daimler COG5s was pursued by BCT's management throughout the mid- and late 1930s. Between the end of March 1935 and 1 May 1935, fifteen metal-framed NCME H26/22R-bodied COG5s were delivered and were a good attempt at the standard pre-war Birmingham outline, but they could be easily identified by having particularly thick upper saloon corner pillars and the neatly rounded cowl under the windscreen – both featured on the then standard NCME bodywork. The bodies were not a great success and were the first batch of COG5s to be eliminated from the fleet – the last going in 1948, with seven of them becoming long-lived lorries in the service fleet. 682 (AOG 682) is parked in Quinton Road West at the terminus of the 10 route in 1947. (D. R. Harvey Collection)

691 (AOG 691)

Above: Coachbuilders went to great pains to gain prestigious orders to meet BCT's exacting requirements. In February 1935 Short Brothers delivered five metal-framed bodies on Daimler COG5 chassis. 691 (AOG 691) was the first bus in the BCT fleet to have a complete repaint after the end of the Second World War. 691 is standing at the 11 route bus stop outside Cotteridge tram depot in Pershore Road on 14 July 1945, opposite George Mason's grocery shop on the corner of Watford Road. These were the last Short Brothers bodies ordered by the undertaking as the company totally changed over to manufacturing aircraft during the following year. The bodies were easily identified by the curved guttering over the front upper saloon windows. They were also the last buses to be fitted with an Autovac above the bonnet on the bulkhead. (J. E. Cull)

726 (AOP 726)

Below: MCCW-bodied Daimler COG5 AOP 726 is posed at the end of June 1935 before the number plate was relocated from the bottom of the slightly angled radiator to the cream panel below the windscreen. This official photograph shows the latest subtle developments in BCT bus design over the previous two years. There is only a small amount of gold lining left out on the paintwork below the driver's cab. 726 was sold to Liverpool Corporation on 7 November 1947 after the Green Lane depot fire in 1947 that destroyed forty-seven tramcars, becoming their D508 for the eleven months it was operated on Merseyside. (BCT)

757 (AOP 757)

Above: In August 1937 an immaculate 757 (AOP 757) crosses Navigation Street as it travels towards the city, past the hidden Queen's Drive entrance to New Street railway station and along Hill Street on the 31A service from the Gospel Lane loop in Acocks Green. In the distance a 1925-vintage Brush-bodied EMB Burnley bogie 40-hp tram – 711 – loads up in Hill Street on the 39 route to Alcester Lanes End. The BRCW-bodied 757, with its bonnet lined out in gold paint and its polished radiator, has a radiator slipboard, which could be altered to give extra information to intending passengers. (G. H. F. Atkins)

773 (AOP 773)

Below: About to turn out of Hill Street in front of the main entrance to the post office and into Victoria Square is BRCW H30/24R Daimler COG5. It was only a few weeks old here, having entered service on 1 July 1935. It is working on the 24 route from Warstock, with the radiator slipboard showing that it is travelling via Showell Green Lane. The thick upper saloon front corner pillars, square front windows and relatively flat front with a slightly protruding destination box are characteristic features of the BRCW body design. (W. J. Haynes)

94 (BOP 94), Daimler COG5, 9531, MCCW, H28/24F, 11/1935

BOP 94 was the Daimler exhibit 1935 Olympia Commercial Motor Show. Wearing BCT livery, BOP 94 was a one-off fifty-two-seat front entrance MCCW-bodied Daimler COG5 (body contract 105) with a Gardner 5LW 7.0-litre engine. It was built in order to test the concept of the front entrance and staircase double-decker, a layout successfully introduced by Midland Red in 1934 with their SOS FEDD vehicles. It was withdrawn on 31 October 1950 and in January 1951 was sold to Bird, Stratford-upon-Avon, for scrap.

94 (BOP 94)

94 (BOP 94) was exhibited at the 1935 Olympia Show when its MCCW fifty-two-seat, four-bay construction body had a little more gold lining out. It had a forward staircase and an entrance with a sliding door that was always locked in the open position. 94 was demonstrated to BCT between 27 August 1936 and 30 November 1936 when it was purchased as 94. It spent its entire life working from Acocks Green Garage on the 1 and 1A routes. It amassed almost 270,000 miles during its fifteen-year career. 94 is at the 1A terminus in Acocks Green village outside the New Inns public house in 1949. (D. R. Harvey Collection)

94 (BOP 94)

Loading up with passengers on 2 May 1950 in St Mary's Row, Moseley, is the Daimler COG5 front entrance former demonstrator 94 (BOP 94). The semi-streamlined rear of the bus had a centrally positioned emergency door with a window on either side of the door and a single window as the upper saloon emergency exit. The rear destination box was set very high and making it difficult for the conductor to change destination displays. (A. D. Packer)

827 (BOP 827)

Above: On 6 November 1950, 827 (BOP 827) stands on the forecourt of Birchfield Road Garage, which became the home of many a geriatric BCT bus over the years. At this time Birchfield Road Garage was the last to have petrol tanks, resulting in the last of the petrol–engined Brush wartime rebodied AEC Regent 661s being allocated there. At the end of December 1950, this Daimler COG5 entered service on 5 October 1936 and although rebodied with the BRCW body from 806 in October 1948, it was withdrawn on 30 November 1952. (R. Wilson)

836 (BOP 836)

Below: Standing alongside the recently abandoned tarred-over tram tracks in Alum Rock Road is Birmingham RC&W-bodied Daimler COG5 836 (BOP 836). The 55A bus service was the direct successor to the former 8 tram route, but it was now a shortworking of the newly extended 55 bus route to Shard End. It turned around at the distant island at the Pelham Arms, a 1920s mock-Jacoban council estate public house that stood at the junction of Alum Rock Road and Pelham Road. In 1951, BOP 836 is at the Bundy Clock prior to returning to the city from alongside the single-storey Co-operative grocery store. It was withdrawn on 30 November 1952 and was one of the last BRCW-bodied buses from this 1936 class to be withdrawn. (E. Chitham)

846 (BOP 846)

Above: Liverpool Street Garage was opened in September 1936. Judging by the pristine state of the garage floor it was only a few days later that these three positively gleaming, almost brand-new Daimlers stand near to the fuel pumps at the Liverpool Street end of the garage. MCCW-bodied 846 (BOP 846), 854 (BOP 854) and the distant BRCW-bodied 819 (BOP 819), the newest of the three, which entered service two months later than the MCCW-bodied COG5s on 21 September 1936, wait to be parked up before their next duty. In the distance is one of the six Guy Conquest C single-deckers that had been taken out of service in January 1936. (D. R. Harvey Collection)

869 (BOP 869)

Right: Barford Street Garage was opened in June 1925 and was always associated with the Inner Circle 8 route. It was closed in April 1955 when its work was reallocated after the opening of Lea Hall Garage. The 8 route's duties were taken over by nearby Liverpool Street Garage. 869 (BOP 869), a 1936 Daimler COG5 with an MCCW H30/24R bodywork, is parked at the exit to the garage before setting off to work on the high-intensive 8 Inner Circle route on 19 June 1938. (D. R. Harvey Collection)

926 (COH 926)

Opposite above: Leaving the bus stop opposite the Kings Head public house in Hagley Road, Bearwood, 926 (COH 926) is working into the city centre on the 9 route. What at first sight seems to be an ordinary Metro-Cammell-bodied Daimler COG5 is far from that. It was one of just four buses fitted with the top deck from a Metro-Cammell-bodied Morris-Commercial Imperial; in this case from 520, due to the original top deck being destroyed in an air raid in December 1940. The replacement hybrid body was eventually transferred to 926 in February 1946. Except for the body framing in the upper and lower saloons not matching and the upper saloon front corner pillars being much narrower than on post-1933 Metro-Cammell, deliveries only the lack of upper saloon mouldings and the painted blue bands between the decks look wrong. In this guise COH 926 lasted until 30 November 1949 before being taken out of service. (S. E. Letts)

953 (COH 953)

Opposite middle: Working on an 11 route shortworking to Acocks Green is an immaculate MCCW H30/24R-bodied Daimler COG5 953 (COH 953), having been returned to service on 1 May 1958 after being in store for up to four years. This was one of the forty-one COG5s that was repainted and overhauled. It was used by Acocks Green Garage on shortworking duties until 31 December 1959. As 953 is turning from Vicarage Road, All Saints Church (completed in 1899) can be seen peeking out from behind the churchyard trees into Alcester Road South in Kings Heath. (F. W. York)

1012 (CVP 112)

Opposite bottom: Prior to entering service on 1 July 1937, along with another twenty from the 968–1033 class of Metro-Cammell H30/24R-bodied Daimler COG5s, 1012 (CVP 112) was posed for the official BCT photograph of the batch. Immaculately presented with a chromed radiator, the bus would not have a long life: after an accident it was withdrawn quite early on 31 October 1949. (BCT)

1023 (CVP 123)

Below: As a Midland Red SOS QL turns into Hill Street in August 1937, BCT's 1023 (CVP 123), an immaculately presented Daimler COG5 with a MCCW H30/24R body, crosses the Navigation Street junction when only a few weeks old. It is travelling into the city along Hill Street on the 15A service from Barrows Lane, Yardley. It has the bonnet lined out in gold paint and its sparkling, polished radiator is carrying a radiator slipboard. (G. H. F. Atkins)

1027 (CVP 127)

The majority of bodies built for BCT's huge Daimler COG5 fleet were constructed by Metro-Cammell and were largely withdrawn by 1955. A reserve fleet of forty-two buses were stored and in 1957, due to the takeover of the College Road and Walsall Road routes, Metro-Cammell-bodied Daimler COG5s were overhauled and put back into service, to be spread around the garages in threes and fours in order to allocate newer buses to these two important arterial road routes operated from Miller Street Garage. 1027 (CVP 127) was one of the buses to be returned to service in September 1958, and in the twilight of its career is being used on a shortworking of the 44 route in Warwick Road when crossing the junction at Baker Street. The bus had been first withdrawn in January 1954 and was stored as a snowplough for three years. It was finally withdrawn on 31 December 1959. (F. W. York)

1139 (DON 439), Daimler COG5, 10350, MCCW, H30/24R, 12/1937

This Daimler COG5 was exhibited at the 1937 Commercial Motor Show at Olympia with a highly polished engine and chassis. The chassis number for 1139 was completely out of sequence with all the contemporary COG5 and had the usual Gardner 5LW 7.0-litre engine. Its MCCW H30/24R body was the solitary one in the bodybuilders' contract 173. Numerically it was the first bus of the 1938 contract, but it received a body built to the earlier 1937 style.

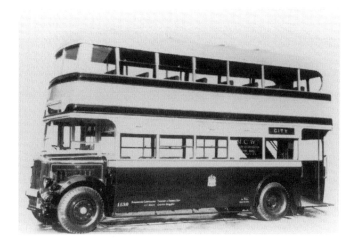

1139 (DON 439)

In around 1950 1139 (DON 439) stands in Hob Moor Road near the Green Lane junction in Little Bromwich, quite close to the City Sanatorium Hospital, and is working on the 16A cross-city service to Handsworth Wood. By now recently fitted with the 1937 body from 1128, DON 439 was taken out of service on 30 April 1954. (D. Barlow)

1938 EOG series

Above: Under construction at Metro-Cammell are at least ten of the soon-to-be EOG-registered Daimler COG5s. The buses are approaching completion in the late summer of 1938 and will shortly go to be painted. In the distance are a number of six-wheeled Leyland trolleybuses for London Transport. (D. R. Harvey Collection)

1139 (DON 439)

Opposite below: The only Daimler COG5 bus to have an odd registration was 1139. A decision was made by Daimler that one of its Metro-Cammell-bodied Birmingham buses should be exhibited at the 1937 Commercial Motor Show at Olympia, so an extra chassis was built. As a result, the next batch of fifty chassis was reduced by one, so that 101 (EOG 101) never existed and the 1,938 deliveries from Metro-Cammell were apparently one short. 1139 was duly exhibited but with a body style from the 1937 CVP-registered batch, retaining the guttering around the front upper saloon windows that was omitted on the EOG-registered buses. Despite its superior exhibition finish, 1139 still weighed the normal 6 tons 16 cwt. The MCCW advertisement in a lower saloon window states that the body was of 'PATENTED METAL CONSTRUCTION SEATING CAPACITY 54'. (BCT)

119 (EOG 119)
Left: Waiting to leave the Old Square in around 1948 when working on the 14 route to Kitts Green not long after being repainted is 119 (EOG 119), a 1938-built Daimler COG5 with a 1939 MCCW H30/24R body from 1196 (FOF 196). The EOF batch of bodies were a further development of the standard BCT body, having larger upper saloon windows without front guttering and deeper rear windows on both the platform and the upper saloon emergency window. (E. Chitham)

153 (EOG 153)
Above: The 1938 BRCW bodies also had the latest design modifications, which rather emphasised the very square-shaped ledge below the windscreen. The BRCW-bodied COG5s also had slightly deeper edges to both canopies over the platform and the engine bay. The body construction was not as good as the MCCW-bodied examples, resulting in earlier withdrawal. 153 (EOG 153) is parked in Washwood Heath Garage yard in 1949, a year before its withdrawal. (D. R. Harvey Collection)

1169 (FOF 169)

Right: Almost completed! 1169 (FOF 169) stands in Metro Cammell's erecting shop in July 1939 at the head of a line of London Transport six-wheel chassisless L class seventy-seater trolleybuses. It is only lacking the nearside mudguard and its registration plate. This Daimler COG5 entered service on 1 August 1939 and was withdrawn on 31 October 1949. It met an unusual end as it was last seen in Bruges, Belgium, as a slightly lowered engineless trailer. (MCCW)

1261 (FOF 261)

The last pre-war-style bodies were thirty built by BRCW on Daimler COG5 chassis and were delivered between 1 September and 1 November 1939. A well-laden 1261 (FOF 261) is in Edgbaston Park Road just after the abandonment of the Cannon Hill trams on 1 October 1949 and is on a shortworking of the 1 route to nearby Moseley village. All the bodies built by BRCW and MCCW in 1938 and 1939 omitted the guttering over the enlarged upper saloon front windows. (S. N. J. White)

8

One-off Bodies in 1939 on Daimler COG5 Chassis

The intended closure of the Birmingham tram system was intended to be in the summer of 1944 and, with the numbers of new buses required, other coachbuilders were approached to provide a prototype body to BCT's requirements.

1237 (FOF 237), Daimler COG5, 10848, EEC, H30/24R, 1/3/1940
Daimler COG5 1237 (FOF 237) was bodied by English Electric, who had been a major player in tram bodybuilding in the UK. This was another speculative bus body and, like the body built on the Imperial 505 (qv), no order from BCT was forthcoming. It was withdrawn on 30 April 1954.

1237 (FOF 237)
Although having supplied Birmingham with piano-front bodies on AEC Regents in 1930, by the end of the 1930s EEC were gaining only a small number of orders for its standard body design. Numerically, 1237 (FOF 237) was the first of the one-off bodies ordered in 1939. 1237 had a well-proportioned English Electric BCT-style body, which was rather spoiled by the blue-painted front apron to the cab. 1237 stands in Martineau Street on the recently abandoned tram tracks in around 1951 when about to leave on the 33 service to Kingstanding. (R. A. Mills)

1237 (FOF 237)
Parked outside K. Lefkaritis' offices in Herman Street, Famagusta, on the Mediterranean island of Cyprus on 13 August 1955 is 1237 (FOF 237). Registered TP 832, the English Electric body has been cut down and the whole of the upper saloon removed, along with the staircase, giving a seating capacity of thirty. The upper saloon floor has wooden rails around it in order to carry virtually anything around the local villages in the Famagusta and Nicosia area, including chickens and goats. Lefkaritis bought twenty double-deckers from BCT via Birds and cut them down to single-deckers where they lasted for up to around twelve years. The destination board reads 'Lefkaritis' in Greek. (D. R. Harvey Collection)

1238 (FOF 238), Daimler COG5, 10831, Park Royal B5640, H30/24R, 1/¾40
1238's Park Royal body had the thinnest front corner pillars of any pre-war body mounted on a BCT Daimler COG5, a rather square destination aperture and a curved profile to the area above the number plate. Inside, it was the only bus in the fleet to have metal-capped window pillars. Withdrawn on 31 July 1951, it was stored until it was sold to Bird, Stratford-upon-Avon, in early September 1954 and exported to K. Lefkaritis, Larnaca, Cyprus, in the same month and re-registered TL 740. The bus was withdrawn in the early 1960s and the remains of 1238 were burnt out by a stubble fire in 1981.

1238 (FOF 238)

Previous page below: Of the three prototype bodies supplied to the Corporation this was Park Royal's interpretation, and it was that firm's first body ever supplied to Birmingham. Their body number B.5640 was allocated to this one-off vehicle and it was a faithful reproduction of Birmingham's standard body, but it must have cost a fortune to develop and build. Alas, no orders accrued. This is the official Park Royal photograph of 1238 (FOF 238) and it still has its bonnet lined out in gold. This was one of the only three diesel-engine buses to be delivered in 1940 – in this case in March of that year. (Park Royal)

1238 (FOF 238)

Left: Loading up at the utility bus shelters in Hagley Road at Five Ways, opposite the old King Edward's School buildings, on Christmas Eve 1949 is Park Royal-bodied 1238 (FOF 238). It is on its way to Quinton on the cross-city 34 route from Kingstanding. This service replaced the 34 tram on 11 August 1930, making it the third Birmingham tram route to be abandoned. (J. E. Cull)

1239 (FOF 239), Daimler COG5, 10833, Brush, H30/24R, 2/12/1939

The third prototype body was on 1239 (FOF 239). It was built by Brush and was on another Daimler COG5. 1239 was one of the last pre-war standard BCT bodies to be built. After withdrawal on 31 August 1950, 1239 went to Birds on 17 January 1951 who then sold it to Hants & Sussex, Emsworth, in March 1951.

1239 (FOF 239)

Posed in the grounds of the Brush factory in Loughborough in November 1939 is Daimler COG5 1239 (FOF 239). The bus had a number of extra embellishments, including highly polished chrome windows in cab area and a chrome radiator surround. The overall effect was that the bodywork, with its radiused saloon windows, looked a much better finished vehicle when compared to the other two prototype bodies that were built. (Brush)

9

The Successful Search for an Alternative Chassis

964–968 were a trial batch of Leyland Titan TD4cs fitted with Lysholm-Smith torque converters, bought to ascertain a suitable chassis as an alternative to the established standard Daimler COG5. They were fitted with Leyland E39/4 8.6-litre diesel engines and had the newly designed Leyland metal-framed H28/24R bodywork, with the original style of square rear dome but a straight staircase and BCT style fixtures and fittings. They all entered service on 1 May 1937. The success of these five buses led to BCT ordering the 135 Leyland Titan TD6c model that were specifically designed for the city's Transport Department.

964 (COX 964)
As an alternative option to the easy change Wilson preselector gearbox with a fluid flywheel on the Daimler COG5, BCT became interested in Leyland Motors' gearless transmission, which trialled on the demonstrator TF 7310. The Corporation purchased five Leyland Titan TD4cs, which had Leyland's own Colin Bailey-designed metal-framed bodies. Bailey had been headhunted from Metro-Cammell in Saltley to design a new metal-framed double-decker as the previous design, introduced by Leyland in September 1933, had been a disaster. The first of these Bailey-designed Leyland bodies for BCT was on 964 (COX 964). It is turning out of Islington Row in May 1938, with the Five Ways Clock showing 2.55 p.m. (D. R. Harvey Collection)

968 (COX 968)

Above: The five Leyland-bodied Leyland TD4c chassis were sufficiently modified to become the prototypes for the new TD5 chassis model. They were in competition with the five AEC Regent 0661s and, with Birmingham's need to dual source its future bus fleet orders, Leyland Motors – perhaps against expectations and logic – won. This resulted in an order for 135 Titan TD6cs for the tram-conversion programme on the two routes to Dudley. 968 (COX 968) looks quite superb prior to delivery in April 1937 and were all withdrawn in 1948 after only eleven years of service. (Leyland Motors) The result of the successful operation of these five 1937-built Leyland Titan TD4c buses is that two batches of 135 Leyland Titan TD6c chassis were ordered, developed specifically to BCT specifications. There were eighty-five TD6Cs, with MCCW H28/24R bodies (contract 196) that were modified to suit the Leyland chassis, and another fifty built with most attractive Leyland bodywork. All had Leyland E39/4 8.6-litre engines and Lysholm-Smith torque converter gearboxes.

249 (EOG 249)

Below: 249 (EOG 249) was one of the twelve Leyland Titan TD6cs to have its body damaged beyond repair during an air raid that badly damaged Hockley Garage on the night of 22–23 November 1940. BCT purchased twenty new English Electric H28/26R units intended for Manchester Corporation and to their streamlined design after their order for Daimler COG5 chassis was largely destroyed when Daimler's Radford Works was bombed and the completed bodies had become surplus to Manchester's requirements. 249 was returned to service in early September 1942 with a new EEC body fitted by Metro-Cammell and lasted until the end of June 1953. It is parked opposite the Uplands public house at the Oxhill Road terminus of the 70 route on 19 July 1951. (G. F. Douglas, courtesy of A. D. Packer)

253 (EOG253)

Above: Parked at the top of Livery Street in 1949 just above the vehicle entrance that led to the main booking office of Snow Hill station is 253 (EOG253), a Metro-Cammell-bodied Leyland Titan TD6c. This bus was first licensed on 1 March 1939 (in time for the tramway conversion of the Handsworth, West Bromwich, Wednesbury and Dudley routes on 1 April of that year) and remained in service until April 1952. Looking in immaculate condition, the body was slightly different to the MCCW bodies on the Daimler COG5s, with a longer front side bay in the upper saloon, while the upper saloon seating capacity was reduced to just twenty-eight. (R. Marshall)

290 (EOG 290)

Below: 290 (EOG 290), like a number of the Metro-Cammell bodied TD6s, was run in at Acocks Green Garage and is posed by BCT in Olton Boulevard East in December 1938 prior to entering service. The slightly longer upper saloon front side bay coupled to the lack of guttering above the upper saloon front windows and the small-sized front tyres made these buses easily identifiable from the contemporary COG5 chassis. The seating capacity of the Metro-Cammell bodies was reduced by two in the upper deck in order to comply with the tilt test requirements because of the added weight of the torque converter gearbox. (BCT)

1297 (FOF 297)

Above: Travelling along Soho Road on its way into the city on the 70 route in around 1950 is one of the attractive Leyland H28/24R-bodied Leyland Titan TD6c 1297 (FOF 297). It had entered service on 1 October 1939 when it was introduced as part of the Dudley Road tram replacement fleet. 1297 was one of the fifty of these handsome-looking buses purchased for the Dudley Road tramway conversion and was in service in time for its opening on 1 October 1939. (S. N. J. White)

1316 (FOF 316)

Below: 1316 (FOF 316) was used for the publicity photographs by Leyland Motors in the autumn of 1939. On Saturday 3 June 1950 this bus is at the stops in Corporation Street between Lower Priory and Bull Street. By now the bulkhead below the front lower window was painted predominantly blue. FOF 316 is operating, fairly unusually, on a cross-city 29 service to Highfield Road, Hall Green, showing that it was one of few of the class to be retained by Hockley Garage when the Ladywood tram service was replaced on 31 August 1947. (G. F. Douglas, courtesy of A. D. Packer)

Trialling AEC Regents

483 (DOB 483), AEC Regent, 6615090, Short, H27/21R, 2/1937
DOB 483 had an interesting history. Its chassis was on loan from AEC to Birmingham City Transport in 1937 and was fitted with the 1930 Short H27/21R body from BCT 483. Registered DOB 483 with fleet number 483, the bus was demonstrated during March and April with an AEC A168 four-cylinder oil engine, thus creating an unofficial Regent 0861 chassis. After the demonstration the body was removed and the chassis returned to Southall. It was then purchased by Provincial as their 42, re-registered DAA 848 and fitted with a Park Royal body.

483 (DOB 483)
Above: After its use in Birmingham the chassis of DOB 483 was sold to Provincial as Gosport & Fareham's 42 and was virtually a new bus. It had a new Park Royal H30/26R body, was re-engined with a six-cylinder AEC A171 oil engine and re-registered as DAA 848. The only clue as to its Birmingham origins was that its chassis number was the first in the sequence of the buses numbered 1034–1038. Birmingham CT had 06615091-5194 and the chassis registered DOB 483 was replaced with a new one numbered 06615149, which became BCT's 1037. Provincial's 42 has just arrived in Gosport bus station. (D. R. Harvey Collection)

1034 (CVP 134)
Overleaf above: Parked in Jardine Road, off Witton Road, waiting for Aston Villa supporters to come out of the match at nearby Villa Park, is 1034 (CVP 134). This was the first of the five AEC Regent 0661s with MCCW H30/24R bodywork. It entered service on 11 July 1937 and remained so until 30 April 1949. The details of the bodywork below the curve to the bottom of the windscreen and the expanse of cream down to the front number plate was significantly neater than on the contemporary Daimler COG5 buses. (R. T. Coxon)

1036 (CVP 136)
Overleaf middle: In their 1930s attempt to purchase buses from a second chassis manufacturer, Birmingham bought five AEC Regent 0661s with Wilson preselect gearboxes. Just two months after the Leyland Titan TD4cs arrived, 1036 (CVP 136) entered service on 11 July 1937 when fuel-consumption trials took place. These buses were allocated to Liverpool Street Garage and, as a consequence, they were regular performers on the Inner Circle route. 1036 is in Lee Bank Road, approaching Five Ways, when new in 1937. It has climbed the steep hill lined with three-storey mid-Victorian terraces that formed a myriad of courtyards and back-to-back slum properties. 1036 was withdrawn on 30 April 1949 and sold in July 1949 to Birds (dealer) for scrap. (J. Cull)

1034–1038

1034–1038 were a trial batch of five AEC Regent 0661s with preselector gearboxes bought in order to test a suitable chassis as an alternative to the established standard Daimler COG5. These Regents had the AEC A173D 7.585-litre diesel engines with a Daimler-type quadrant preselector lever mounted on steering column. They had a standard BCT-designed MCCW body (contract 145), only differing from the Daimler COG5 bodies in the curved design below the windscreen. Their purchase did not lead to any further orders, but it was intended to purchase another fifteen in 1942 as the fuel consumption of the torque converter TD6cs proved to be disappointing.

1038 (CVP 138)

The last of the five Regent 0661s was 1038 (CVP 138), which lasted until January 1951. It stands opposite the Fox & Goose public house in Washwood Heath Road working on a special duty. It is the summer of 1950 and a 762-class bogie tramcar is at the central loading island prior to returning on the 10 route to Martineau Street in the city centre. The MCCW-body Regents had chromed radiators, improving the appearance of these AECs. (T. J. Edgington)

10

Wartime Buses

The Jo'burgs

Other than unfrozen and MoS wartime buses, Birmingham were allocated by the MoWT four 8-foot-wide Daimler COG6s (1320–1323), which were intended for Johannesburg Municipal Transport, South Africa. These were not shipped because of German U-boat activity in the Atlantic Ocean. They were placed in service in an all-over grey livery and were subject to width and height restrictions, resulting in them being initially allocated to Yardley Wood Garage for use on the intersuburban 18 route.

1321 (FVP 921)
Birmingham received four of the five 8-foot-wide Daimler COG5s intended for Johannesburg. They had pre-war H32/26R-styled bodies built by MCCW. The four buses were also restricted to routes where there were no low bridges due to being around 14 feet 8 inches high. 1321 (FVP 921), by now allocated to Harborne Garage, passes through Victoria Square on 30 March 1948 when working on the 9 route along Hagley Road to the Birmingham boundary in Quinton. They were the first buses in the fleet to be delivered with Gardner 6LW 8.4-litre engines. (J. Edgington)

RT19 (FXT 194), AEC Regent III (RT), O6616767, LPTB, H30/26R, 1/1940
LPTBs RT 19 (FXT 194) was new in 1939 and used as an AEC demonstrator between January 1940 and August 1942 to twenty-two operators. It had an experimental AEC A182 engine and a changed rear axle ratio for provincial use. It arrived for its eighteenth period of demonstration to BCT between 7 June 1941 and 7 July 1941. Back with London Transport in 1945, it was fitted with an AEC A185 9.6-litre engine and an air-powered preselector gearbox, which upgraded the chassis to the post-war 3RT chassis specification.

RT19 (FXT 194)
Demonstrating to Nottingham CT in September 1940 is RT 19 (FXT 194). It is in the green and cream livery of Mansfield District Traction, which it wore throughout its two-and-a-half-year period of demonstration. On a really miserable rainy day it is operating on the 31 Mapperley service. In the roof box destination blind the bus carries the AEC badge. (W. J. Haynes)

RT19 (FXT 194)
In post-war livery, RT19 (FXT 194) is parked in Kingston after the vehicle's last overhaul in 1951 and is about to work on the 85 route to Putney Bridge. RT 19 had become something of a guinea pig after 1945, with numerous engine and chassis modifications and body interior upgrading. It was perhaps significant that the largest post-war order for the RT in the provinces came from Birmingham City Transport, who in 1937 had failed to purchase the AEC Regent and were approaching AEC again to supply new chassis just as war broke out. (F. G. Reynolds)

1356 (FOP 356)

Above: There were very few official photographs taken during the Second World War of new BCT MoS-type buses. One of the few was of 1356 (FOP 356), which was unusual in that it arrived in the full BCT fleet livery whereas most of the class were delivered in all-over grey. This Weymann-bodied Guy Arab II 5LW entered service with wooden-slatted seats on 1 March 1944 and has all the wartime blackout additions such as the grey-painted camouflaged roof, headlight and interior light masks and white edging paint on all the bottom edges of the bus. This was one of eighty-four wartime Guys delivered to Birmingham, who also received sixty-five wartime Daimlers. (BCT)

1403 (FOP 403)

Below: This is a line-up of wartime Guy Arab IIs led by 1403 (FOP 403), a brand-new Weymann-bodied Guy Arab II with a Gardner 5LW 7.0-litre diesel engine. The line-up of ten wartime buses is parked outside Yardley Wood bus garage on 1 November 1944. The picture was used for publicity in the local press and it was inferred that these were the latest buses to be delivered. 1403 is seen on its first day in service. In fact, they were not all new and had two different body manufacturers' products. Immediately behind the leading bus is 1376 (FOP 376), another Weymann-bodied Guy Arab II and new in mid-July 1944; the next four are Park Royal-bodied Guys; and the distant, last three are more Weymann-bodied Guys. The chief distinguishing feature of the Weymann body was that the top of the offside cab windows went up almost to ceiling level and was not lined up with the top of the windscreen or the bottom of the canopy. In addition, the front profile of the Weymann body was flat whereas the Park Royal body had a slightly curved profile. (BCT)

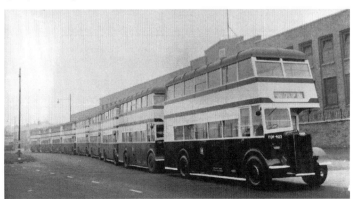

11

Early Post-war Buses and Demonstrators: 1945–50

1235 (FOF 235), Daimler COG5, 10878, MCCW, H30/24R, 16/11/1939
1235 was built with a standard MCCW H30/24R body, but this was transferred to 1231 (FOF 231) on 26 February 1946. 1235 was rebodied with the prototype post-war metal-framed Brush H30/24R double-decker body and re-entered service on 1 May 1946. Brush obtained the order for 100 bodies for the new Leyland Titan PD2/1 chassis, numbered 1656–1755. Delicensed between 1955 and 1957, 1235 was returned to service on 1 September 1957 in time to augment the bus fleet to cover for the route acquisitions from Midland Red. 1235 was finally withdrawn on 31 December 1960 and was operated by Lloyd, Nuneaton, until August 1963.

1235 (FOF 235)
It was perhaps something of a surprise when Brush Coachworks were asked to build the post-war prototype post-war body on the 1939 chassis of 1235 (FOF 235). The metal-framed body structure is virtually complete and, although windowless, some of the lower saloon stress panels are in place and the sides of the upper deck have been panelled. The unfinished structure stands on a dolly truck in the bodybuilder's yard in Loughborough in January 1946. (Brush)

1235 (FOF 235)

Above: Certain features of the 1946 Brush bodywork mounted on the 1939 Daimler COG5 chassis 1235 (FOF 235) were not repeated on future exposed-radiator bus body orders. The deeply recessed windscreen, designed to stop night-time reflections from the illuminated lower saloon, would eventually return in a much modified form on the buses with new look fronts in 1950. One peculiarity was the enormous front and rear destination boxes used for giant destination lettering. This was soon altered by reducing the size of the apertures, although the large front box shape was retained. 1235 also had a twin window upper saloon emergency exit. The newly rebodied bus is parked in the grounds of the Brush factory in Loughborough with the railway viaduct of the former Great Central Railway in the background. (Brush)

1235 (FOF 235)

Below: The similarity between the 1946 Brush body mounted on 1235 (FOF 235) and the 100 supplied by Brush to BCT on Leyland Titan PD2/1 chassis between March 1948 and May 1949 is startling. 1235 is in Dudley Road working on the short B80 route to the city boundary at Grove Lane when allocated to Rosebery Street after its return to service on 1 September 1957. (L. Mason)

As a result of the successful rebodying of 1235, Brush was awarded a contract to body 100 of the earliest Leyland Titan PD2 Sp chassis. Although these metal-framed bodies were some of the best built by Brush, these were the last bodies delivered to BCT due to their failure to meet BCT's design and manufacturing specifications.

1733 (HOV 733)

The driver walks towards the cab of 1733 (HOV733), which is parked at the exit of Perry Barr Garage in around 1963. It is about to work on the cross-city 29 route from The Circle, Kingstanding, to Highfield Road, Hall Green, by way of Hockley, High Street in the city centre and Sparkhill. The Brush body on this Leyland Titan PD2 Sp is remarkably similar to the 1946 prototype body on 1235, though the design of the larger driver's cab is much neater and the whole body sits much lower on the chassis. (D. R. Harvey Collection)

1484 (GOE 484)

1484 (GOE 484) entered service on 4 July 1947 and was seen a few days before this for publicity purposes. The first post-war deliveries were seventy-five Daimler CVA6s powered by an AEC A173 7.58-litre engine. It was a development of the wartime CWA6 model, but had flexible engine mountings. The 7-ton 12-cwt Metro-Cammell H30/24R bodies were unique to BCT. They had the general shape of the new post-war bodies, but these had very thin body pillars and recessed window pans that were not repeated on subsequent MCCW bodies for BCT. This class introduced the raked windscreen, designed to prevent reflection from the lower saloon lights onto the windscreen at night. 1484 was taken out of service on 31 December 1961. (BCT)

Post-war RTs

The culmination of AEC's attempts to gain orders from BCT were the fifteen AEC Regent 0961 RT chassis with 9.6-litre engines and Park Royal bodies delivered between July and October 1947. Numbered 1631–1645, they were allocated to Acocks Green Garage. The body was a Park Royal thin-framed, four-bay design (highly modified to meet BCT requirements) with a long, raked windscreen intended to eliminate reflection. This gave the bus something of a unique frontal appearance, with the headlights not being level and the mudguards being too short. Coupled with a non-standard staircase, air brakes that were always a source of trouble, an air preselector gearbox and a limited route availability, they were fast, fragile and fun to ride on. A five-bay version of this body style was fitted to the 2181–2230 class of Leyland Titan PD2/1s delivered between 1949 and 1950.

1635 (GOE 635)
Above: On a hot summer day in 1949, 1635 (GOE 635) is outside the Warwickshire County Ground in Edgbaston Road. It is working on the 1A route from the city centre via Five Ways, Moseley, and Acocks Green. The AEC Regent III 0961s had standard Park Royal H29/25R bodies coupled to the BCT designed driver's cab, resulting in a somewhat idiosyncratic-looking vehicle, which was not helped by the small 9.00 front tyres. They were also the last buses in the fleet to retain wheel discs, which like their RT cousins in London, were only on the rear wheels. (S. N. J. White)

1642 (GOE 642)
Overleaf above: Passing through Victoria Square with the classically styled Birmingham Council House behind it is AEC Regent III 0961 Park Royal-bodied 1642 (GOE 642) on the 1 route shortworking to Stratford Road, Springfield, in September 1947 only a few days after entering service. They had limited route availability because of their air brakes and air-operated preselector gearboxes, resulting in only Acocks Green Garage drivers being passed out to drive them. They were used only on the 1, 1A, 31, 32 and 44 services, but were rarely used on the 25-mile-long Outer Circle 11 route, partly due to the L-shaped staircase posing problems for unwary passengers. (G. H. F. Atkins)

The PD2s

296 (HOJ 396), Leyland PD2, 470848 (EX2), Leyland, H30/26R, 29/9/1947
296 (HOJ 396) was the second of a pair of prototype Leyland PD2 chassis, the
first being CVA 430. 296 was fitted with O.600 9.8-litre engine and was painted
in full BCT livery. It was the first post-war BCT double-decker to achieve twenty
years in service, being withdrawn on 31 October 1967 and sold to Hartwood
Finance (dealer), Barnsley, in June 1968. 296 had a Leyland PD1-style body, but
had the lower cab apron below the windscreen finishing halfway down the offside
mudguard.

296 (HOJ 396)
Opposite above: BCT had been a valued customer of Leyland Motors in 1938, ordering 135 of
the specially designed Titan TD6c to its own specification. The thinking was that in the post-war
world Birmingham would again use Leyland as its alternative supplier. Thus, the new large
9.8-litre PD2 was seen as an ideal model for Birmingham. Only two PD2 chassis were ever
built, and the second (originally numbered EX2 and the only PD2 to be given a normal Leyland
chassis number) was delivered to BCT and entered service on Monday 29 September 1947 with
the registration HOJ 396. It is standing in Nelson Road, Witton, waiting for the crowds to leave
the 'Temple of Dreams' (the location 'VILLA PARK' is shown on the destination blind). This
prototype Leyland could be easily identified when new as it carried a pair of rather splendid,
large, brass-rimmed PD1-type headlights. The Leyland-painted livery had a thin middle blue
band below the destination box. (D. Griffiths)

296 (HOJ 396)

296 was allocated to Yardley Wood Garage for all its life. It was the only post-war bus to be numbered in the Series 2 sequence, which had last been used in 1939. By 1959 it had been repainted into the standard fleet livery with two full-depth blue bands, and at first glance looked like a member of Hockley Garage's 2131 class. Its registration number plate, unlike the later buses numbered 2131–2180, was below the windscreen while the arrangement of its half-drop upper saloon windows was different. It was the first post-war vehicle to operate for twenty years, achieving 312,000 miles in service. It shows the typical Birmingham 'SERVICE EXTRA' destination display as it travels towards the city, just past Sparkhill Baths in Stratford Road, on 2 May 1963. (F. W. York)

The order for 200 Leyland Titan PD2/1s for delivery between 1948 and 1950 had the body order split three ways, with Brush getting an order for 100 based on the prototype 1235 and Leyland and Park Royal getting orders for fifty bodies each. The Leyland-bodied PD2/1s were numbered 2131–2180 and were direct successors to the body on 296.

2132 (JOJ 132)
This bus was one of the first twenty-three of the class of fifty to be delivered in the wrong livery, with the middle blue line covering the moulding between the decks being reduced to a thin band. 2132 (JOJ 132) was the second bus in a batch of fifty Leyland-bodied Leyland Titan PD2/1s that were delivered in 1949. This glistening new bus stands outside the Hockley Branch of the Birmingham Municipal Bank. (D. R. Harvey Collection)

2144 (JOJ 144)
Loading up with passengers in High Street, West Bromwich, in 1963 when working on the jointly operated 74 route to Dudley is 2144 (JOJ 144). This Leyland-bodied Leyland Titan PD2/1 had by now received the small black fleet numbers on the lower saloon waist rail. Their excellent power-to-weight ratio made them the fastest double-decker buses in post-war fleet. They spent their entire lives based at Hockley Garage, employed on the cross-boundary services through West Bromwich to Wednesbury and Dudley, replacing the pre-war Leyland Titan TD6cs. (A. J. Douglas)

2181 (JOJ 181)
The final fifty Leyland Titan PD2/1s had standard five-bay Park Royal H29/25R bodies that were modified internally with BCT fixtures and fittings. They did have Birmingham external livery moldings and the bodies looked like a five-bay version of the Park Royal bodies mounted on the 1631–1645 class of 1947-built AEC Regent III 0961RTs. 2181 (JOJ 181) is posed for its official photograph in September 1949 and, although built without a straight staircase, looks quite splendid. An interesting aside is that any BCT bus with an exposed radiator whose registration ended in a 1, such as here with JOJ 181, had a number plate that left a gap next to the radiator shell. (Park Royal)

Enter the Crossleys

GNE 247, Crossley DD42/1, 92901, Crossley, H30/26R, –/1944
Although not in chronological order, GNE 247 was on loan from Crossley Motors, Stockport, and was demonstrated to BCT during 1945. This vehicle was fitted with a prototype Crossley HOE7 8.6-litre engine, had a Brockhouse torque converter and was operated in the then current Manchester Corporation art deco, streamlined red and white livery. It was returned to Manchester CTD and numbered 1217 at an unknown date.

1217 (GNE 247) had not long returned to Manchester Corporation after it had been demonstrated and inspected by numerous operators, including Birmingham City Transport when it was seen on the 48 route to Altrincham. As a demonstrator it retained Manchester's startling streamlined 'swoop and droop' red and white livery. The body had been intended for 1211 but, as a new body, post-war prototype was not ready then this one was substituted. The bus differed from all other Crossleys by having a tall, high-mounted radiator but with a thin radiator surround. (Crossley Motors)

DJA 434, Crossley DD42/7, 94933, Crossley, H30/26R, –/1949
Partly as a result of the successful demonstration of GNA 247 in 1945, plus Crossley
having the capacity to fulfil a large order of buses (albeit to Birmingham specification
rather than Crossley's standard product), DJA 434 arrived in the city in the spring
of 149 for driver training purposes. This was a Crossley DD42/7 chassis with one of
the three prototype downdraught HOE7/5B 8.6-litre engines fitted to a double-deck
chassis. The bus had a four-bay Liverpool-style Crossley H30/26R body. It went on
a brief demonstration to BCT for familiarisation purposes in May 1949 before 1655
(GOE 655) 94804 was delivered. In November 1949 it was sold to Clynnog & Trevor
Motor Co., Trevor, Caernarvonshire.

DJA 434
Opposite above: The former Crossley Motors demonstrator DJA 434 was sold to Clynnog &
Trevor in 1949 and stands in the shadow of Caernarfon Castle in Castle Square in front of the
Castle Hotel. This DD42/7 had the improved downdraught HOE7/5B engine, which was similar
to those used in half the large order to BCT, but had the attractive four-bay Crossley body
developed for Liverpool Corporation. (R. F. Mack)

DD42/6

Above: The order for 270 Crossley DD42/6 with Crossley bodies was delivered in sixteen months. The buses were designed to the exacting requirements of BCT and had little in common with the contemporary chassis or bodies being produced by Crossley Motors. Although seemingly just one order, there were five variations in the series. There were ten prototypes, numbered 1646–1655 and registered GOE 646–655. 260 production vehicles quickly followed and was worth well over £1 million. The final part of the order was numbered 2426–2525 and was mechanically identical but had the BCT-designed, new look concealed radiator. Crossley then allocated another 100 chassis numbers for an anticipated repeat order, but this was not placed by BCT and the chassis numbers 95201–95300 remained unused.

1647 (GOE 647)

Below: The almost new 1647 (GOE 647) is lying over in Church Road, South Yardley, opposite the Yew Tree public house, having worked on the 15A route. 1647 entered service on 11 June 1949 and was finished to exhibition standards. Its body was the first in the BCT fleet to have sliding ventilators and fitted with decorative wheel trim discs on the front and rear wheels. It still has its original thin-top radiator, which were unique to this batch of ten. This bus was fitted with one of the three more powerful pre-production prototype HOE7/5B downdraught engines supplied in this group of ten buses to BCT and, as such, was the prototype for the 2396–2425 class of exposed-radiator Crossleys. On the right is 1362 (FOP 362), a 1945 Daimler CWA6 with a Duple body that is in its last year in service. (D. Griffiths)

1655 (GOE 655)

Above: 1655 (GOE 655) waits at the South Yardley terminus of the 15B route in Garretts Green Lane at the junction with Sheldon Heath Road in September 1949. It was the first of the new BCT Crossley chassis numbered 94801 and, along with all future GOE-registered chassis, was stored in Liverpool Street Garage before returning to Crossley Motors to be bodied and in the case of 1655, uniquely fitted with the third prototype HOE7/5B downdraught 8.6-litre engine but coupled to a Brockhouse-Salerni turbo-transmitter torque-converter gearbox. 1655, a DD42/6T, could be identified by the oil reservoir for the turbo-transmitter mounted on the front bulkhead. Entering service on 7 September 1949, it was less than successful, having a constantly revving engine, a lot of whirring and a distinct lack of forward motion. The torque-converter gearbox was removed on 18 September 1951 after having covered 48,901 miles. (D. Griffiths)

2325 (JOJ 325)

Left: Passing the main entrance to Snow Hill railway station in Colmore Row is 2325 (JOJ 325), which is working in 1959 on the 31A route to Gospel Lane in Acocks Green. This was one of the first eighty of the production batch of Crossley DD42/6s with 8.6-litre Crossley HOE7/4B engines and half-drop saloon windows. 2325 was always allocated to Acocks Green Garage, being first licensed on New Year's Day 1950 and withdrawn on 31 March 1966. (F. W. York)

2419 (JOJ 419)

Right: On 10 August 1950, after just nine weeks in service is 2419 (JOJ 419). About to load up with passengers in Old Square, this gleaming Crossley DD42/6 is working on the 43 service to Nechells. This was the former 7 trolleybus route that was abandoned because of its failure to be able to comply with the wartime blackout regulations. 2419's Crossley body was fitted with sliding saloon ventilators and was one of the last exposed radiatored buses delivered to BCT and was equipped with the new uprated Crossley HOE7/5B 8.6-litre downdraught engine. In the distance in Steelhouse Lane is the Gaumont Cinema. (G. F. Douglas, courtesy A. D. Packer)

2489 (JOJ 489)

Above: 2489 (JOJ 489) stands in Lordswood Road alongside the 1905-built Kings Head public house. 2489, sporting its decorative front and rear wheel discs, waits for its leaving time at Bundy Clock when working on the Outer Circle 11 route. The bus, which had the improved Crossley HOE7/5B downdraught engine, had a very solidly built Crossley H30/24R body weighing 8 tons 6 cwt 2 qtrs. 2489 entered service on 1 July 1950 and was one of the last of a hundred Crossley-bodied Crossley DD42/6s that had the new look concealed radiator. 2489 remained in service until 31 March 1969. In 2020 it will have been in preservation in this condition for fifty-one years. (G. Burrows)

The First Guys

2526–2625, JOJ 526–575 were modified Arab III chassis to BCT specification. Thus, Arab III Sp is a shorthand method of defining the 301 chassis built for BCT between 1950 and 1954. They were fitted with Gardner 6LW 8.4-litre engines, a preselector Wilson epicyclic gearbox and the BCT-designed new look concealed front. Chassis FD 70192 was the prototype Birmingham specification Guy Arab chassis, which was used for testing behind normal service buses in Birmingham during late 1949. The chassis was returned to Guy Motors after these tests and broken up in 1952.

Chassis FD 70192
Above: This was a chassis prototype to BCT's exacting specification, variously designated Birmingham-Guy, Guy Arab III, BCT Arab, IIISp or Arab IV. The chassis was used in Birmingham where it shadowed normal service buses from Quinton Garage and its all-round performance was thoroughly monitored. The chassis had a wheelbase of 16 feet 4 inches and had a fluid flywheel coupled to an epicyclic preselector Wilson gearbox with a floor-mounted gear change lever coupled to a Gardner 6LW 8.4-litre engine. It incorporated a new look concealed radiator and did not have a rear platform chassis extension. A Birmingham chassis, parked at Fallings Park, reveals that both the fuel tank and the vacuum tank for the triple servo braking system were located outside the chassis frame but between the wheelbase. (D. R. Harvey Collection)

2640 (JOJ 640)

Bought for the Coventry Road trolleybus route conversion on 1 July 1951, 2626–2775 were all Daimler CVD6s with Daimler CD6 8.6-litre engines and were the start of a new era for the development of Birmingham's bus fleet. These MCCW-bodied buses were the first in the fleet to be 27 feet long, with the extra length being used to enlarge the platform area. All previous Birmingham metal-framed body orders had the bodies built in two halves, but these buses were the first standard BCT design to have one-piece, metal-framed bodywork (identifiable by the lack of between-decks guttering), while the depth of the windows in each saloon was increased. It also had a curved lower saloon bulkhead window behind the bonnet. As an economy measure, the rear platform had rubber matting instead of strips of ash and a lot of the interior moquette was replaced by leather. Brand-new 2640 (JOJ 640) stands in Albert Street outside the Beehive department store when about to leave for Sheldon on the replacement 58 service beneath the trolleybus overhead, which is yet to be cut down. (D. R. Harvey Collection)

The Final Tram Replacement Buses: Crossley-bodied Daimler Cvg6s and Guy Arab IVs

Many of the last traditional-looking Crossley-bodied Daimler CVG6s and Guy Arab IV Spl 6LWs with Metro-Cammell bodywork delivered to Birmingham City Transport were used in the final closure of Birmingham's last tram routes.

2779 (JOJ 779)

Overleaf above right: The first body-only contract built by Crossley were for 125 vehicles mounted on Daimler CVG6 chassis, thirty-three of which were used in the conversion of the Bristol Road and Cotteridge tram services on 5 July 1952. The bodywork was very well finished, though some cost cutting in the specification meant that the bodies were constructed in one piece – easily identifiable by having no external guttering below the middle blue livery band. 2779 (JOJ 779) was actually in service on 3 May 1952 and remained in use, latterly by WMPTE, until 31 December 1974. (Crossley Motors)

3021 (MOF 21)

Left: On the Saturday morning of the abandonment of Birmingham's last group of tram routes, brand-new buses were sent out of Miller Street to Aston Road North and passengers were taken off the tramcars and put on to the new buses between Aston Cross and Victoria Road. 3021 (MOF 21), showing 'OK' in the destination number box, is in Aston Road travelling out to the exchange point on 4 July 1953. A distant redundant tram has just come out of service and is returning to Miller Street depot before making its last journey that afternoon to Kyotts Lake Road Works for eventual scrapping. (H. Sergeant)

3121 (MOF 121)

On the afternoon of 4 July 1953, with the final ceremonial trips by trams 616 and 623 to Erdington earlier that morning, 3121 (MOF 121), one of the Crossley-bodied Daimler CVG6s, is unloading passengers outside the nurses' home of the General Hospital in Whittall Street. It is working on the new replacement 64 bus service and will shortly turn left into Steelhouse Lane where it will load up before returning to Erdington. (S. N. J. White)

Early 1950s Single-decker Demonstrators

99 (LRW 377), Daimler Freeline G6HS, 25001, Duple B30+30D, 9/1951
Fitted with a Gardner 6HLW horizontal 8.4-litre engine, the Daimler Freeline underfloor-engined single-decker was their answer to the heavyweight Leyland Royal Tiger and AEC Regal IV chassis. LRW 377 was numerically the second Freeline chassis to be built.

The chassis was completed in April 1951 and was sent to Duple, receiving a two-door standee layout bus body with electric-operated doors and forced ventilation. It was painted in Edinburgh Corporation livery and to their specification. LRW 377 was demonstrated to BCT between 29 March and 29 May 1952.

99 (LRW 377)
Above: During its two-month trial the Freeline (LRW 377) seems to have been exclusively operated on the long 28 route. This ran between Station Street in the city centre to Great Barr by way of practically every suburb on the eastern and northern sides of Birmingham. The 28 route was deemed suited to this experiment with a standee single-decker, as it had high-peak-time traffic and a low suburban ridership at all other times. It is at the terminus of the 28A bus route in Dyas Road at the Glenmead Road turning circle during April 1952. This two-door Duple-bodied Freeline had only thirty seats in a 2 and 1 split, and room for thirty standing passengers. Birmingham's bus passengers made unfavourable comments about there being not enough seats! (R. Knibbs)

OTD 301, Leyland Tiger Cub, PSUC1/1 515177, Weymann Hermes B44F, 7/1952
This was one of the first prototypes of the Tiger Cub chassis. It had air brakes and a neat-looking Weymann body, but within a year this body was fitted to a new chassis, numbered 520001, re-registered as RTB 49 and sent on its way as a demonstrator again. Its appearance between 1 and 16 December 1952 was therefore one of its comparatively rare outings in this guise.

OTD 301

OTD 301 is at the impressive bus shelters in Church Road, Northfield, on a bleak day in December 1952 when working on the 27 service. This was one of the few single-deck-operated routes in Birmingham due to low railway bridges at Northfield and Bournville. Having travelled from West Heath to Northfield, it will progress to Bournville and Stirchley before arriving at the terminus in All Saint's Road, Kings Heath. Its lightweight construction, coupled to the small Leyland 0.350 horizontal 5.7-litre engine – which, after all, was why the Tiger Cub model was developed in the first place – would have counted against it in Birmingham. Additionally, the Tiger Cub was initially only offered with a constant-mesh gearbox and was not popular with the drivers in BCT's easy change fleet. (S. Palmer)

12

Experimental Buses

The Golden Years of Birmingham Demonstrators

88 CMV, AEC Regent V, MD3RV, MD3RV001, Park Royal H33/28R
88 CMV was the first AEC Regent V to be built, being completed for the 1954 CMS as a Crossley Regent V with the chassis number CMD3RV.001; although, originally, it had the chassis number U.168623 in the experimental series. The MD series of Regent Vs had a lightweight chassis and was powered by an AEC AV 470 7.685-litre engine with a four-speed synchromesh gearbox and air brakes. It had an attractive green and cream painted 8-foot-wide four-bay Park Royal H33/28R medium-weight body. It was demonstrated to BCT between 25 March and 15 April 1955.

88 CMV
88 CMV was in Birmingham for just three weeks and, like all the vehicles demonstrated to the undertaking, was allocated to Lea Hall Garage. The 14 service to Tile Cross estate was used for all the vehicle trials as it was considered the best one that combined all the Corporation's service characteristics. 88 CMV stands at the city terminus in Old Square in April 1955 when about to leave on the 14 route to Kitts Green. 88 CMV was the first of three 27-foot-long demonstrators to be trialled, but within a year shorter demonstrators with lower seating capacity were at a disadvantage as new legislation enabled 30-foot-long chassis to be put into service. (A. Yates)

159 JHX, AEC Regent V, MD3RA, MD3RA298, Park Royal H37/28R, b. 6/1956
159 JHX was ACV's first attempt to get a major order from BCT since 1931. The bus
was operated in a predominately blue version of the Birmingham livery and had a
BCT triple-indicator destination display. Originally it had a four-speed synchromesh
gearbox, but before its third visit to the city the chassis was fitted with an air-operated
monocontrol epicyclic gearbox, thus becoming a MD2RV chassis. 159 JHX was
demonstrated to BCT between 26 June and 21 July 1956, returning during January
1957. It returned again between 18 March and April 1957 and was subsequently sold
to R. Chisnell, 'King Alfred', Winchester, in September 1958.

159 JHX
AEC really tried to get an order from Birmingham with its small-engined AEC Regent V 159 JHX,
built specifically for use in the city. It paid three visits to the Corporation and had two different
types of gearbox. 159 JHX has just arrived from the city centre on the 14E route in April 1957.
After the livery fiasco with the AEC Q in 1933, one might have thought that the very attractively
styled Park Royal body might have been painted in the correct livery by ACV! (W. S. Godden)

SDU 711, Daimler CVG6, 18954, Willowbrook, H37/27R(D), –/1955
SDU 711 was built for the 1955 Scottish Commercial Motor Show and had a
Willowbrook H37/27R body built directly on to the chassis without an underframe. A
similar batch of fifteen buses was bought by Walsall Corporation in 1956. The result was
a body with an overall height of just 14 feet while retaining a high-bridge layout. It was
fitted with a Twiflex centrifugal clutch instead of a fluid flywheel. It was demonstrated
to BCT between 23 January and 20 February 1957, and after being used extensively
elsewhere as a demonstrator it was sold in April 1960 to S. Ledgard, Armley, Leeds.

SDU 711

Standing on the forecourt of Lea Hall Garage in January 1957 is the low-height 27-foot-long Willowbrook-bodied demonstrator SDU 711. The Twiflex centrifugal clutch gave a conventional friction drive but with an automatic engagement, thus giving better fuel economy than a bus with a fluid flywheel. The four-bay sixty-six-seater body was fitted directly on to the chassis. The result was a bus not only with a lower height but also noticeably lower mounted and shallower saloon windows below the waist rail. It had the characteristic Willowbrook recessed upper saloon front windows with air ventilators. Built with rear-entrance doors, they were left open while the bus was in Birmingham. (D. Williams)

3228 (9 JML), Crossley Bridgemaster, MB2RA, MB2RA002, Crossley H41/31R, 2/1957

There were five prototype low-height integral Bridgemasters, and this was the second Crossley-bodied example to be built. 9 JML was exhibited in the Demonstrator Park at the 1956 Earl's Court CMS and was the first 30-foot-long bus to be demonstrated to BCT. 9 JML came to BCT between 13 February and 1 August 1957 and was used to test a 30-foot-long, 8-foot-wide double-decker on a busy radial route. The bus had the small AEC AV 470 7.685-litre engine coupled to a four-speed synchromesh gearbox and was purchased by BCT in September 1957, becoming fleet number 3228. The Crossley body had a H41/31R layout but was only allowed to operate after an agreement with the T&GW Union, stipulating that the platform staff would only collect fares if there were no standing passengers. This trailblazing agreement presaged the 'no standing rule' on all BCT's subsequently purchased 30 footers. On 9 March 1965, the larger AEC AV.590 9.6-litre engine was fitted. 3228 was withdrawn in June 1969.

(9 JML)

Above: When 9 JML first came to Birmingham in February 1957 it was still in the green and white demonstration livery worn in October 1956 in the Demonstrator Park at Earls Court. It was not modified when it arrived to work the 14 route, but had a special blind made to fit the single-aperture destination box. The attractively bodied Crossley Bridgemaster is turning back to the St Giles Road terminus at the traffic island at Tile Cross Road in March 1957. It is displaying an 'ON HIRE TO BIRMINGHAM CITY TRANSPORT' sticker in the lower saloon front window, while the legal ownership is displayed on the first nearside panel as 'AEC Ltd, Southall, Midd'x, Miss G. L. Knight, Sec't'. 9 JML was a good buy, but its rear air suspension made for a rather too bouncy a ride; however, the real Achilles heel, as with all Bridgemasters, was not having a semi-automatic gearbox and while the AEC manual gearbox was one of the easiest to drive, the bus was still quite hard work. (D. R. Harvey Collection)

3228 (9 JML)

Below: Still retaining its Crossley Coptic Cross radiator badge, 3228 (9 JML), as it had become, stands in the still unfinished reconstruction of Old Square in the spring of 1963 and is about to turn left into Corporation Street when working on the 14E route to Kitts Green. The high driving position on the Crossley Bridgemasters was well disguised by the slightly lower-mounted AEC Regent V radiator cowling and the well-proportioned Crossley bodies. The bus had been painted in what was to become Birmingham's blue and cream livery with two narrow blue bands. (D. R. Harvey Collection)

VKV 99

Above: VKV99 stands in the Old Square at the terminus of the 14E service to Kitts Green in July 1958. Of all the demonstrators that came to Birmingham in this period, this bus perhaps came nearest to the traditions and requirements of the Transport Department. It was a 30-foot-long and 8-foot-wide open rear platform Daimler with preselector transmission, seventy-four seats and, to cap it all, a Birmingham new look front. The attractive Willowbrook seventy-four-seater body was an extended version of the low-build high bridge body first seen on SDU 711. Unfortunately, Willowbrook bodies were never the most robust of products, and the flimsy translucent roof drummed and vibrated quite badly over some of the inner-city cobbled road surfaces. (S. N. J. White)

VKV99, Daimler CVG6-30, 30001, Willowbrook, H41/33R, 4/1957
The first 30-foot-long demonstrator to be operated by BCT was VKV 99. This was the second 30-foot-long Daimler CVG-30 to be built and was exhibited at the 1958 CMS. It had a Willowbrook low-height H40/34R body that was a 30-foot-long version of that built on SDU 711. Along with Walsall Corporation's 824 (YDH 224), it was the only CVG6-30 to have a Birmingham-style, new look concealed radiator. VKV99 had an 18-foot 6-inch wheelbase and originally had a Gardner 6LW engine, but in 1958 it was re-engined with a Gardner 6LX 10.45-litre unit. It was used by BCT between 23 June and 15 July 1958 and in 1961 was sold to McGill, Barrhead.

2211 MK, AEC Bridgemaster 2B3RA, 2B3RA067, Park Royal H43/29F, 5/1960
2211 MK was the first forward-entrance AEC Bridgemaster 2B3RA to be built and was made specifically for demonstration in Birmingham. It was fitted with a rather austere metal-framed Park Royal H43/29F body that was considerably lower than the normal post-war BCT bus. Equipped with an AEC AV 590 9.6-litre engine, 2211 MK was demonstrated to BCT between 14 June 1960 and 2 May 1961. In March 1961 it was seen carrying the fleet number 3229, suggesting that it was going to be purchased; however, it was sold to G. W. Osborne of Tollesbury, Essex, later that year.

2211 MK

Above: With its paintwork still gleaming from the Park Royal paint shops, 2211 MK is at the Kitts Green terminus of the 14E route in July 1960 at the beginning of an eleven-month stay in Birmingham. It was an AEC Bridgemaster 2B3RA and was the sixty-seventh AEC Bridgemaster to be built and was the first to have a forward entrance. The appearance of the ungainly steel-framed Park Royal H43/29F body rather detracted from the quality of the vehicle. The interior of the Park Royal bodywork trialled various body features that were to be found on later Daimler Fleetlines with yellow ceilings and an interior trim that was to become standard on post-1962 deliveries. A small window was located just in front of the set-back front entrance doors. 2211 MK was the last conventional front entrance bus to be demonstrated to BCT. (D. R. Harvey Collection)

2211MK

Below: Parked at the Kitts Green terminus of the 14E route is 2211 MK the prototype front entrance Park Royal-bodied AEC Bridgemaster 2B3RA. It was kept as a demonstrator for eleven months and it was seen with the fleet number 3229 for a short period. The rather ugly Park Royal bodywork was developed for the BET Group of bus companies (S. N. J. White)

OHL 863, Guy Wulfrunian, FDW 6LX, FDW74407, Roe H43/32F, 10/1959
The first Guy Wulfrunian chassis was FDW74407 and was first registered in November 1959 as OHL 863 then exhibited as West Riding's 863 at that year's Kelvinside Scottish Commercial Motor Show. The Guy Wulfrunian was built at the request of Ronald Brooke West Riding Automobile's Fleet Engineer, requiring a maximum-capacity modern double-decker, a front entrance and overhanging front platform. OHL 863 had independent air front suspension, Dunlop disc brakes and a drop rear axle providing a lower chassis in order to pass under low bridges and be able to cope with the arduous and rough operating terrain of Wakefield and the surrounding areas.

OHL 863
Above: OHL 863 is parked in Congreve Street outside the Birmingham Transport Department's offices on 6 November 1959 and is awaiting inspection by BCT's General Manager. The Wulfrunian had a Roe H43/32F body and is in West Riding's livery. OHL 863 was fitted with a chromed radiator, but this was a feature that was not repeated on any subsequent Wulfrunians. The model had a heavy a front-mounted Gardner 6LX 10.45-litre engine, resulting in a very cramped driver's cab and poor access to the engine for the engineering staff. Of the 137 Wulfrunians built, 126 went to West Riding and six more were acquired second hand. (L. Mason)

8072 DA, Guy Wulfrunian, FDW 6LX FDW74443, Roe H41/31F, 6/1960
Guy Wulfrunian 8072 DA was exhibited at the 1960 CMS and was intended to be Guy Motors' high-capacity answer to the rear-engined Leyland Atlantean and the Daimler Fleetline. It was a front-engined, front-entrance, double-decker chassis, but the advanced experimental features of the design had received insufficient development, resulting in severe operational difficulties with the suspension, brakes and non-power-assisted steering. With the heavy Gardner 6LX 10.45-litre engine overhanging the front axle, drivers had to have almost Herculean strength to manoeuvre it. The attractively styled Roe bodywork had a rear ascending staircase on the nearside, causing congestion on the platform at peak periods. 8072 DA, registered thus because of its seventy-two seats, was demonstrated to BCT between 8 and 16 July 1960.

8072 DA
This was the second Wulfrunian to be built from a production run of only 137. Loading up with passengers when operating on the 14E service in Old Square in July 1960, 8072 DA has the old gold and black livery of its home town's football team, Wolverhampton Wanderers FC. The independent front suspension pulled the front wheels inwards either when under load, as in this case, or if the large rubber air units became deflated due to a fault. This new chassis was just one step too far and effectively bankrupted Guy Motors. The Wulfrunian was a design with too many features being placed into one new chassis design. It would be another twenty-five years before a similar layout was tried again – on the Volvo Ailsa B55. (L. Mason)

46 LTB, Leyland Atlantean PDR1/1, 590548, MCCW H44/34F, 10/1959
The examination of 46 LTB, a Metro-Cammell-bodied Leyland Atlantean PDR1/1 demonstrator, over two days from Thursday 28 January 1960 resulted in the long-term demonstration of 460 MTE a month later in February 1960. 46 LTB was the third Atlantean demonstrator and had the rare distinction of having three registrations during its life: HZA 723 with CIE, 8985 XI with UTA and finally UI 8616 after its sale to Londonderry & Lough Swilly Railway in 1960 as their 87.

46 LTB
With a BCT trade plate in the nearside windscreen, 46 LTB awaits the once over by members of the General Manager and the Transport Committee. It is parked in Congreve Street outside the Transport Department's offices, having been examined by BCT engineering staff in Tyburn Road on the previous day. This Leyland Atlantean PDR1/1 created a sufficiently good impression and showed that rear-engined buses were the way forward as they were able to accommodate over seventy-plus passengers. (D. R. Harvey Collection)

3230 (460 MTE), Leyland Atlantean PDRI/I, 591487, MCCW H39/32F, 2/1960

460 MTE was the fourth demonstrator Leyland Atlantean PDR1/1 to be built and was quickly converted from the original Leyland 0.600 9.8-litre engine to have the bigger Leyland 0.680 Power Plus 11.1-litre engine. This revolutionary design with its transversely rear-mounted engine, Pneumocyclic gearbox and entrance in front of the front axle made the front-engined 30-foot-long double-decker obsolete at a stroke. Originally it had a seating capacity of only seventy-one, but it soon became a seventy-six-seater. One of the few concessions to Birmingham's specification was the fitting of the standard front destination box layout. It was demonstrated to BCT between 21 September 1960 and 1 May 1961, when it was purchased and given the fleet number 3230. 460 MTE had the same bright yellow and pale blue pastel interior that was pioneered on 2211 MK, but it took a long time for this style of bus to gain acceptance by the people that mattered – the passengers!

(460 MTE)
Above: Dropping off passengers in Tile Cross, 460 MTE is working on the 14 route. The Atlantean is in full BCT livery with crests and the only clue that it is a demonstrator is the small notice at the top of the nearside windscreen and its lack of fleet number. The drivers for all Lea Hall Garage's demonstrators were specially chosen, but even they had difficulty with gear changes as they could not hear the rear engine from the cab. The result was that quite often the gear changes were poor, which in turn threw passengers about and made their first impressions increasingly unfavourable. Passengers also had to get used to finding the entrance; it took a few of years before they stopped walking to board at an imagined door at the rear. (S. N. J. White)

(460 MTE)
Right: Turning out of Northbrook Street into Dudley Road when still working as a demonstrator to BCT is 460 MTE. It has the 'on-hire' stickers in the nearside front windscreen and therefore has no fleet number. This MCCW-bodied Leyland Atlantean PDR1/1 is working on the short 95 service back to Birmingham in 1960. (L. Mason)

7000 HP

Above: 7000 HP is on the Daimler exhibition stand at the 1960 CMS in full BCT livery. At this time, 7000 HP still had its original Daimler CD6 8.6-litre engine, which was quickly removed on its arrival in Birmingham as it was quiet but underpowered. It has always been rumoured that because of Birmingham's willingness to allow Daimler to have 7000 HP back as a demonstrator, the pre-production batch of ten (3241–3250) were purchased on extremely favourable terms. The body on 7000 HP was built by Weymann and had a H39/33F layout that was soon altered to H44/33F. The body had slightly recessed window pans when compared to the pre-production batch of ten Fleetlines. (Quadrant)

7000 HP, Daimler Fleetline RE30, 60000, Weymann, H39/33F, 9/1960

Surely one of the most significant buses ever built. The very first Fleetline, 7000 HP, chassis number 60000, was built by Transport Vehicles (Daimler) as a direct competitor to the Leyland Atlantean. It had a transversely mounted rear engine, a Daimatic epicyclic gearbox and a drop-centre back axle. The overall height of the bus was then reduced by around 6 inches and could have a central gangway in both saloons. The intention had been to allocate the prototype Fleetline with the registration 3229 VP, inferring that it would receive the fleet number 3229 in the BCT fleet, but Daimler requested the bus for an energetic sales push around the country and the bus duly received the Coventry registration 7000 HP, but as a demonstrator retained its BCT's livery. It was used by BCT between 9 December 1960 and 31 January 1961.

3238 (238 DOC)

Loading up a couple of passengers in All Saints Street on the railway bridge at Hockley Goods station over the old GWR mainline is 3238 (238 DOC). As a result of the demonstration of 460 MTE, ten Leyland Atlantean PDR1/1s with Leyland 0.680 Power Plus 11.1-litre transverse rear engines and bodied by MCCW with H39/33F layouts were purchased and all entered service on 5 November 1961, being numbered 3231–3240 (231–240 DOC). For comparison purposes, ten Daimler Fleetline CRG6LXs were purchased. The Leylands had Pneumocyclic gearboxes, a front entrance and a generously low seating capacity of only seventy-two – the maximum that the unions would then allow. At 8 tons 9 cwt 3 qtrs, they were exactly 1 cwt lighter than 3230. These were the last Birmingham buses to have tungsten interior light bulbs and had the standard BCT front destination box layout with the addition of a small 'TO/FROM CITY' box in the large gap between the thin blue livery band and the bottom of the destination box. (L. Mason)

7000 HP

Below: Parked at the Tile Cross terminus of the 14 route is 7000 HP, the prototype Daimler Fleetline CRG6LX. The bus was distinguished by having a large, fluted Daimler badge on the front panel of the MCCW body, whose height when compared to 460 MTE is noticeably lower. (S. N. J. White)

13

Trying Out Single-deckers

FXE 892C, Bedford VAM5, 13/64/4, Strachan B46F body, 7/1965
There was a change in the control of Birmingham, with the new majority also having power over the Transport Committee. After a change in local government politics, a Conservative-led council led to a new sweeping-clean policy, with ideas such as the development of Limited Stop services and the increasing use of single-deckers. The first single-decker demonstrator was a Bedford VAM5, which was tried on the 4 service. The lightweight chassis had a forward-mounted Bedford 330 5.42-litre diesel engine, a five-speed synchromesh gearbox and three steps into the saloon. It was demonstrated to BCT between 25 November 1965 and 26 February 1966 by Vauxhall Motors, Luton.

FXE 892C
The bus labours up Hillmeads Road as it leaves the Pool Farm terminus of the 4 route in December 1965, on a route for which it was perhaps not best suited. With a manual gearbox, a small engine and a lightweight Pacesaver II body by Strachan, FXE 892C was also tried out on the even shorter 20 service between Northfield and Weoley Castle, where it was set against the contemporary larger rear-engined demonstrators. (A. D. Broughall)

R192s

As a result of the demonstration of the Bedford VAM5, somewhat perversely Birmingham City Transport ordered twelve Ford R192 single-deck buses numbered 3651–3662, albeit with similar Strachan bodywork, which was worth around £48,000. The chassis were fitted with 32-foot-4-inch-long, forty-five-seat bodies built by Strachans (Coachbuilders) to their Pacesaver Mark II design, with lightweight steel frames, double-skinned panelling and with front entrances. These were the first lightweight single-deck chassis to be ordered by Birmingham.

3656 (JOL 656E)

The Limited Stop 99 service was introduced on 3 April 1967 and was only operated in the morning and evening peak periods. The route covered the normal 63 service along Bristol Road between Navigation Street and Rubery, and 3656 (JOL 656E) is parked at the Bristol Road South terminus in Rubery. The buses had three steps and the engine cowling to negotiate, but the Fords were fast and well suited to Limited Stop services. (L. Mason)

FGW 498C, AEC Swift, MP2R 001, Willowbrook B53F, 11/1965

This was the first AEC Swift MP2R to be built. It was fitted with an AEC AH505 8.2-litre small engine that was mounted at the rear. FGW 498C had a four-speed electro-pneumatic monocontrol semi-automatic gearbox. The Willowbrook body was designed to the standard BET style and had a single platform step leading into the flat but ramped saloon floor. It was demonstrated by AEC to BCT between 22 December 1965 and 2 January 1966.

FGW 498C

Left: FGW 498C worked over the Christmas and New Year period of 1965 and was painted in a predominantly bright red with the waist rail, window surrounds and flashings in pale cream. It was evaluated on the 20 route between Northfield and Weoley Castle at the same time as the similar specification Leyland Panther PSUR1/1R when a direct comparison of the two was made. FGW 498C is demonstrating to Crosville Motor Services at Upton-by-Chester early in 1966. It was later sold to Gelligaer UDC as their 35 in 1967. (E. A. Allison, courtesy of J. Carroll)

3678 (KOX 678F)

Above: The outcome of the AEC Swift demonstration in 1965 was the purchase of twelve 33-foot-long and six 36-foot-long MCW-bodied, two-door buses. Entering service in October 1967, the longer ones were the 2P2R model and had the AH691 11.3-litre horizontal engine. The MCW B37D+39 bodywork had an extra half-length window in front of the central doorway. They were purchased for use on routes where the peak-hour business was very busy while off-peak use was limited. The 36 route was the first to be converted, and 3678 (KOX 678F) is lying over in Olton Boulevard West on the 36F shortworking in 1968. Within months complaints from passengers about these 'Crush loading' single-deckers used to a seat and not a strap resulted in no more being purchased. (L. Mason)

HWU 641C, Bristol RELL6G, 222.103, ECW, B54F, 9/1965

Introduced in 1962, the Bristol RE was the first of the 1960s rear-engined chassis to enter production and was fitted with a Gardner 6HLX 10.45-litre engine. This ECW B54F body had the original curved windscreen and rounded rear dome, while the chassis came from the early 222 RE chassis sanction. HWU 641C was demonstrated to BCT between 9 and 16 January 1966 by Bristol Commercial Vehicles prior to delivery to West Yorkshire Road Car as their SRG 15.

HWU 641C
Above: The rear-engined Bristol RELL6G demonstrator worked on the newly introduced 20 service, which travelled the short length of Shenley Lane from just outside Northfield to the terminus at Somerford Road. Saturday 15 January 1966 was a miserable day as HWU 641C stands in the turning circle outside the Weoley Castle public house, with Shenley Lane separating the bus from the distant multistorey flats in Long Nuke Road. With its Gardner engine it created a favourable impression, but it was decided to look elsewhere as Bristol buses, only available on the open market since 1965, still had an unproven track record outside the BTC Group. (B. W. Ware)

STB 957C, Leyland Panther, PSUR1/1R, L22985, Willowbrook B53F, 10/1965
The rear-engined Leyland Panther PSUR1/1 was introduced in 1964, being initially developed for Leyland's customers in Belgium and the Netherlands. The Willowbrook body was very similar to one fitted to the AEC Swift demonstrator FGW 498C. It was demonstrated to BCT between 21 January and 1 February 1966 and sold to Gelligaer UDC as their 36 in 1967.

STB 957C

Previous page bottom: Wearing its demonstration livery of black and white and proudly proclaiming that it is the 'LEYLAND REAR ENGINED PANTHER', STB 957C is working on the 20 route and is parked at the turning circle at Somerford Road, Northfield, on 24 January 1966. The high floor line of the Willowbrook-bodied bus contrasts with the low driving position. The stepped-frame chassis had a Leyland 0.600 9.8-litre engine fitted at the rear. The Panther was to be ordered by BCT as their preferred type of high-capacity single-deckers for OMO use, but Leyland Motors could not meet the stipulated delivery date, resulting in the order going to AEC for their Swifts chassis. (D. R. Harvey Collection)

CVC124C, Daimler Roadliner SRC6, 36002, Marshall B50F, 11/1964

This was the third Daimler Roadliner SRC6 to be built, numbered 36002 and was the first to be bodied as a bus. It was fitted with a rear-engined, compact Cummins V6.200 9.63-litre engine. The chassis was exhibited at the 1964 CMS and the complete Marshall-bodied vehicle was shown at the Scottish Motor Show. It was demonstrated to BCT between 8 and 17 February 1966 by Daimler Transport Vehicles and remained as a demonstrator with Daimler until 1968.

CVC 124C

Above: Of all the single-deck demonstrators tried out by BCT in 1965/66, CVC 124C looked the most attractive. The Marshall B50F body with the standard BET-style front and rear domes, windscreen and rear windows seemed to sit a little lower than on any of the other rear-engined chassis and had an almost-flat floor line, with a lower saloon window level. If ever a bus was ruined by its engine, this was the prime example. Working on the short ride up Shenley Lane on the 20 service in Northfield between 8 and 17 February 1966 revealed that the Cummins engine sounded like dustbin lids being banged together; to the passengers it smelled of leaking engine oil and to anyone in the vicinity it left behind a lovely blue smoky haze as it clattered along the road. It is crossing Bearwood Road at the Bear Hotel when on hire to Midland Red working on its 214 service to Brandhall. (A. E. Hall)

TBU 598G

Opposite above: Parked in Birmingham's Tyburn Road Works in early 1969 is the Seddon RU demonstrator TBU 598G. Having been examined by BCT engineers, it is about to be tilt tested. No orders were placed with Seddon, which was perhaps just as well as too many inherent faults were observed as the Pennine bodies were found to be rather too lightweight and tended to crack around the chassis mounting points and around the centre exit door. This original demonstrator went to Green Bus Service of Rugeley in 1971 and was sold in 1974 when Midland Red took them over. (D. R. Harvey Collection)

TBU 598G, Seddon RU, 44992, Pennine B43D, 3/1969
The initial Seddon RU prototype TBU598G was registered in March 1969 and
had a Pennine Coachcraft forty-one-seat dual-door body on the short-wheelbase
16-foot-6-inch version of the chassis. It had a rear-mounted 10.45-litre Gardner
6HLX driving directly via a fluid flywheel into a self-changing, five-speed, air-operated
epicyclic gearbox and electrical control. The body was a jig-built aluminium-framed
structure and, because of its lightweight construction, was prone to failure while the
chassis had major faults with overheating, vague steering and poor brakes.

NAG 589G, Bristol VRTSL6G, VRT-SL 224, ECW, H43/34F, 9/1969
The Bristol VR chassis was built as a competitor to the Leyland Atlantean and
Daimler Fleetline. In July 1967 Bristol introduced the VRT, which had a transversely
mounted Gardner 6LX engine. This was coupled to a semi-automatic transmission by
self-changing gears. The double-decker had an overall length of 31 feet 2 inches and a
body with a capacity for over seventy passengers. The neat, if rather functional, ECW
body with design characteristics from the earlier front-engined Bristol Lodekka model
shows that this was a Series 1 VRT and sported rather plain flat windscreens.

NAG 589G
Right: Right to the very end of
Birmingham City Transport's existence,
before being taken over by West
Midlands PTE on 1 October 1969, the
undertaking was looking at alternative
sources of double-decker chassis. One
such option was the rear-engined
Bristol VRT. In the summer of 1969,
NAG 589G was inspected in Quinton
Garage by the Garage Manager, several
mechanics and a couple of drivers. As
yet undelivered to Western SMT as their
2238, it is tempting to speculate that the
WMPTE order for 200 Bristol VRTs
was as a result of this visit. (L. Mason)

14

Birmingham Buses at Exhibitions and Being Used as Demonstrators

ON 1125, AEC 507, 507001, Short, H28/22RO, 11/1925
ON 1125 was exhibited at the 1925 Show at Olympia, London, in full BCT livery and to a full Birmingham specification. It was never operated by BCT. It had AEC five-type 6.8-litre petrol engines. It was registered by Birmingham Corporation Transport in November 1925 and was on demonstration from AEC Limited, Southall, in November 1925. ON 1125 was sold to Doncaster Corporation (53) in October 1926 and was withdrawn in 1935.

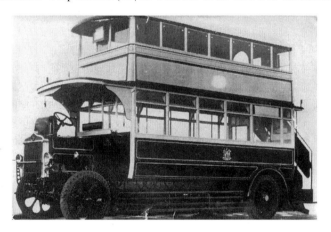

ON 1125
ON 1125 was the first AEC 507 chassis to be built. The chassis, sometimes known as the Ramillies, had an AEC five-type 6.8-litre petrol engine and had a wheelbase of 15 feet 9½ inches long, some 3 inches longer than the previous 504 model. It had a pressed-steel chassis rather than the flitched version of the old 504 type. ON 1125 received a full BCT type Short H28/22RO body and was registered by Birmingham Corporation Transport in November 1925, but was rejected by BCT as being too expensive at just over £1,700 for the completed bus. AEC sold it to Doncaster Corporation as their 53 during October 1926. Eventually some 126 AEC 507s were delivered to BCT between February 1927 and February 1929. (D. R. Harvey Collection)

94, BOP 94

After it was exhibited at the 1935 CMS, BOP 94, the front entrance Daimler COG5, was purchased by BCT at the end of November 1936.

94 (BOP 94)

94 was photographed by BCT in November 1936 when it was yet to be fitted with destination blinds but immediately after receiving its fleet number. (BCT)

1603 (GOE 603)

1603 (GOE 603), a Daimler CVG6, has just been delivered to Tyburn Road Works from Metro-Cammell's Elmdon factory and still has their advertising poster in the front lower saloon offside window. It is late December 1947 here and it would enter service on New Year's Day 1948 from Highgate Road Garage. The earlier members of the class were the last in the fleet to have a handrail across the upper saloon front windows. (A. N. Porter)

1822 (HOV 822), Daimler CVD6, 13979, MCCW H30/24R, 8/1948

1822 (HOV 822) was chosen, along with five other double-deck buses built by Daimler, to travel to Copenhagen in Denmark for British Festival Week in 1948. The six buses were away on this Continental goodwill visit from between 30 August and 12 October 1948. The buses travelled in convoy overland from Dunkirk through the still war-ravaged Belgium and northern Germany and then operated a free bus service around the Danish capital. 1822 was a Daimler CVD6 with a Metro-Cammell H30/24R body to BCT's current design.

1861 (HOV861)

Overleaf middle: Standing in Metro-Cammell's yard in January 1949 is 1861 (HOV861). Differing only by lacking interior handrails across the upper saloon windows and guttering over the staircase window from the GOE-registered batch of CVG6s, many of these Daimler CVG6s had a service life of twenty years and led a very hard life slogging around the very busy Inner Circle 8 route. In the background is the chassis and lower saloon frame of a six-wheeled BUT 9641T trolleybus intended for London Transport. 1861 would stay in service until the end of February 1968. (D. R. Harvey Collection)

1822 (HOV 822)

Landing from a pontoon ferry after having crossed the River Ems from the Netherlands into Germany on its way in convoy to Copenhagen for a British Week is 1822 (HOV 822). It is being followed off the ferry by SHMD's 40 (KMA 510) – one of three Brush-bodied Daimler CVD6s on the trip. 1822 always carried a commemorative plaque on the front bulkhead to recognise this momentous trip to Denmark. (D. R. Harvey Collection)

1933 (HOV 933)

1933 (HOV 933) was the 1949 Earls Court CMS exhibit on the Daimler stand and represented the last-ever exposed radiator class of bus built for BCT by Daimler.

1933 (HOV 933),

Left: Turning into Bull Street from Corporation Street when about to work a football extra to the Hawthorns is 1933 (HOV 933), a Daimler CVD6 with a MCCW H30/24R body. It had been delivered from the exhibition in time for the conversion of the Moseley Road group of tram routes on 2 October 1949. (R. F. Mack)

2033 (JOJ 33), Daimler CVD6, 15715, MCCW H30/24R, 10/1950
The only clue that 2033 (JOJ 33) had ever been anything other than just an ordinary one of the latest concealed radiatored 100 Daimler CVD6s bodied by Metro-Cammell H30/24R was that it was fitted with a curved chrome-plated strip on the top of the bonnet cowl, just above the BCT radiator badge. This piece of additional trim was put on the bus as extra embellishment when it appeared at the 1950 Commercial Motor Show at Earls Court.

2033 (JOJ 33)
The Daimler CVD6 2033 (JOJ 33) still sporting its bonnet embellishment for the 1950 show is about to cross Vicarage Road, Kings Heath, from Avenue Road when on its way to the nearby terminus of the 2 route in All Saints Road in around 1958. It had always been operated by single-deckers due to the low railway bridge not far behind the bus in Dads Lane, but when this was lowered in 1949 double-deckers could just squeeze under the bridge. (D. R. Harvey Collection)

New Post-war Leyland Single-Deckers

The first post-war single-deckers ordered to replace the pre-war Daimler COG5s were thirty Weymann B34F-bodied Leyland Tiger PS2/1s and five integral construction Leyland Olympic HR40 underfloor-engined single-decker buses. They had the large 9.8-litre Leyland 0.600 engine and were fast, economical and long-lived.

2234 (JOJ 234)
Overleaf above: 2234 (JOJ 234) was the Leyland Tiger PS2/1s used for the official Weymann photograph at the end of June 1950. They operated on the long and busy 27 inter-suburban service, which also had low railway bridges in Dads Lane, Kings Heath, Bournville station and at Northfield station. In their early years they were hired out for summer seaside excursion work to Midland Red. The ordering of these buses was something of a mess. Firstly, the order was placed with MCCW for thirty-five buses, but they couldn't build them at Elmdon or Washwood Heath. Then the order was changed to thirty with five of the new underfloor Leyland Olympic HR40s substituted instead. Finally, BCT tried to get the PS2 order altered from 27 feet 6 inches to 30 feet in order to take advantage of the new legal length for single-deckers that was about to come available, but it was too late to alter the body length. Despite these early problems, these 6-ton, 18-cwt, 1-qtr heavyweights had long lives and four of them are preserved. (Weymann)

2265 (JOJ 265)

Above: This was the first underfloor-engined single-decker bus to be built by Leyland Motors. A total of only twenty-three of this integral HR40 model were ever built, and they were only 27 feet 6 inches long and 7 feet 6 inches wide. BCT had five of them, which was the largest batch to be produced. They had Leyland horizontal 0.600 9.8-litre engines and with Weymann B36F bodies, which had riveted panels into the frames and the floor line marked with a decorative polished strip. The interior had aluminium-faced window cappings, but otherwise was completed to normal BCT standards. All were converted to OMO in the autumn of 1963 when the seating capacity was reduced to thirty-four. The last of the five was 2265 (JOJ 265), which entered service on 1 September 1950 and was the subject of the official Weymann photograph. (Weymann)

Crossley's Moment of Glory

2516 (JOJ 516), Crossley DD42/6, 95188, Crossley, H30/24R, 10/1950

ACV approached Birmingham's General Manager about exhibiting one of their latest all-Crossley new look fronted buses at the 1950 Commercial Motor Show at Olympia. Having agreed to the request, 2516 was chosen and, after going back to BCT, it ran for nearly six months. In the spring of 1951 ACV approached BCT for the second time as this time they would like to exhibit 2516 again at the prestigious Festival of Britain at the South Bank site in London as an example of 'British Bus Building Excellence'. Again, this was agreed, but Mr W. Smith insisted that despite being little more than six months old 2516 must be completely repainted, overhauled and given a complete set of new tyres – all at ACV's expense.

2516 (JOJ 516), Crossley DD42/6 2516 (JOJ 516), exhibited at the 1950 CMS, is parked on show at the Festival of Britain on 18 July 1951. It is seen sparkling in the summer sunshine and sporting a small extra chrome strip over the top of the concealed radiator. (S. Palmer)

A Tested Daimler

Although never used in service, a 1951 Daimler CVD6 2726 with an MCCW H30/24R body was experimentally fitted with a Daimler CD650 10.6-litre supercharged engine by Daimler, who then used it as a test bed on the fearsome hills in Halifax, although not in passenger service.

2726 (JOJ 726)

2726 (JOJ 726) entered service on 1 October 1951. It had a Daimler CD6 8.6-litre engine, but in 1956 it was used as a test bed for their new CD650 10.6-litre supercharged engine carrying trade plates 084. The re-engined bus is parked in Halifax bus station. (D. R. Harvey Collection)

The Lightweights

With dropping passenger numbers, more expensive fuel and increasing wage bills, thought was given to trialling lightweight buses but with bodies to BCT specification. Three were purchased between 1952 and 1954. 3001 was a Guy Arab IV; 3002 was one of only two Daimler CLG5 to be built; and 3103, a Daimler CVG6, had a lighter standard body.

3001 (LOG 301), Guy Arab IV Spl 6LW, FD 71252, Saunders-Roe, H30/25R, 10/1952

3001 (LOG 301) was the first of three experimental lightweight buses to enter service. The Corporation became interested in reducing costs and, rather like the rest of the British bus industry, began to realise that many of the buses in production were over-engineered, had poor fuel consumptions and were very heavy. Guy Motors took out of the assembly line one of the JOJ batch of Arab IVs chassis that was modified by fitting lighter components. This bus had the chassis number FD71259, which would have placed it around 2960 in the previous class of MCCW-bodied Guy Arab IV Spls. The Saunders-Roe body, built at Beaumaris, Anglesey, had a lightweight floor/ceiling unit between the saloons linked to the main body frames and weighed 7 tons 4¼ cwt – around 17cwt lighter than normal.

3001 (LOG 301) stands in the main hall of Earls Court prior to the opening of the 1952 Commercial Motor Show. This unique Saunders-Roe bodied Guy Arab IV had a Gardner 6LW and its Saunders-Roe body was a remarkably good copy of the standard Birmingham style, but it had aluminium window pans and aluminium interior bulkhead cappings and lighter seat frames. It lacked the upper saloon guttering above the windows and could be distinguished from the front by the slightly more prominent front route destination box. Unfortunately, as Saunders-Roe could not guarantee being able to meet the delivery date for 100 bodies, the contract was awarded to MCCW. The body, on which Saunders-Roe must have spent a small fortune in development costs, did however last for almost twenty years. (D. R. Harvey Collection)

3001 (LOG 301)

Being overtaken by a Ford V8 Pilot in Victoria Square is Saunders-Roe-bodied 3001 (LOG 301). When new it had a Gardner 6LW engine, but this was exchanged for the smaller second-hand 5LW unit in mid-June 1953 as the bus had a somewhat lively power-to-weight ratio. As 3001, working on the 31A route to Gospel Lane, Acocks Green, has yet to be fitted with the Coronation flag holders beneath the front destination blind, it must still have the larger Gardner engine. (S. Palmer)

3002 (LOG 302), Daimler CLG5, 18335, MCCW, H30/25R, 10/1954

3002 (LOG 302) was the second of only two genuinely experimental lightweight Daimler CLG5s chassis that were completed; the other becoming REH 500, bought by PMT, were chassis that were sold to their respective operators to test. LOG 302 was fitted with a Metro-Cammell H30/25R body that was a cross between the previous Aurora body and the Orion, which was about to go into production. The complete bus weighed only 6¾ tons and had weight-reducing aluminium-covered interior window-cappings, bulkheads and lightweight seats. A unique feature was the sliding cab door, which added a touch of modernity to an otherwise austere appearance.

3002 (LOG 302)

Opposite above: 3002 stands in Congreve Street at the 1A route's city centre terminus opposite the Transport Department's offices located in the Council House extension in around 1958. 3002 looked different from the more usual BCT 'tin front' double-decker, having rubber-mounted same-depth saloon windows and a pair of slatted lower saloon front bulkhead air ducts. The windows in each saloon gave it an airy look, but although it had all the accoutrements of a Birmingham bus, its saloon windows and its almost vertical rear dome and small emergency window made it stand out as something different. Its body was prone to drumming and, in its early years, was stiffened to remedy the problem. The three lightweight buses were to be just as much a developmental cul-de-sac as Birmingham's last two tramcars, 842 and 843, which ironically enough were also lightweight. (R. F. Mack)

3103 (MOF 103)

Left: 3103 (MOF 103) was the third lightweight-bodied BCT bus with a Crossley H30/25R body on a Daimler CVG6 chassis. This was the most standard-looking of the three buses and had a lighter version of the standard Crossley body that weighed 7 tons 4 cwt, making it comparable to 3001, but still 9 cwt heavier than 3002. Entering service in June 1954, it had Auster pull-in ventilators in the upper saloon front windows and opening side ventilators in the rear dome windows. The body had riveted panels, aluminium-covered interior window cappings and lightweight seat frames and yet still retained twin-skinned interior upper saloon domes. The chassis number, 18173, would have placed it as 3112 had it received a normal Crossley body, but due to its experimental construction and materials it was delivered some eleven months late. It is parked at the Oxhill Road terminus of the 70 route in front of the Uplands public house when new in 1954. (D. Griffiths)

Daimler CVG6s and Guy Arab IV Spl 6LWs

A number of the last Crossley-bodied Daimler CVG6s and Guy Arab IV Spl 6LWs with Metro-Cammell bodywork were also used by their respective chassis manufacturers as demonstrators at the end of 1953 and the early months of 1954. Undoubtedly the successful demonstration of the Daimlers led to orders in Chesterfield, Coventry and Glasgow, whereas Guy Motors failed to get any benefit from their efforts.

3017 (MOF 17)

Opposite above: The bus chosen for the official photograph for the MOF series of Metro-Cammell bodied Guy Arab IV Sp with Gardner 6LW 8.64-litre engines was 3017 (MOF 17). This bus was first licensed for service on 1 July 1953, in time to be used on the conversion of the three Erdington tram services four day later. These buses, as with all those delivered after the summer of 1951, were built as one-piece bodies, slightly deeper saloon windows and more interior leather cloth coverings (D. R. Harvey Collection)

3060 (MOF 60), Guy Arab IV Spl 6LW, FD 71757, MCCW H30/25R, 11/1953

Above: 3060 (MOF 60) is working on the 11 route on a dreich day in January 1954 – not Birmingham's famous Outer Circle, but the one in Glasgow. 3060 (MOF 60), which had entered service on 1 November 1953, is at the Yoker terminus bespattered with mud when it was being demonstrated, operated by Knightswood garage. It was also briefly used by AA Motor Services in Ayr. A second MCCW-bodied Guy Arab IV Spl, 3080 (MOF 80), was also sent directly to Glasgow in January 1954 before entering service in Birmingham during the following month. (J. Thomson)

3132 (MOF 132), Daimler CVG6, 18226, Crossley H30/25R, 7/1953

Overleaf above: Although Coventry was the home of Daimler, the problem for Coventry Transport was that the municipality had never operated a bus equipped with a Gardner 6LW 8.4-litre engine. Birmingham City Transport's Daimler CVG6 3132 (MOF 132), with a Crossley H30/25R body new in July 1953, was used with its Birmingham municipal crests removed as a demonstrator by Transport Holdings (Daimler), Coventry, to Coventry Corporation from 15 December 1953 until 28 December 1953. The following month it fulfilled the same purpose with Glasgow Corporation. On its last day of demonstration in Coventry, MOF 132 turns out of the still incomplete Broadgate when working on the 21 service to Alderman's Green. The trial with this bus was successful and led to a total of 171 of the CVG6 chassis being ordered by Coventry Transport. (T. J. Edgington)

3180 (MOF 180)

Left: Parked up in Witton tram depot on 28 March 1954 are 3180 and 3181, a pair of Daimler CVG6s with Crossley H30/25R bodies, along with a number of other members of the class. 3177 to 3206 were delivered some months earlier but were stored in the old tram depot until the spring of 1954 as they were surplus to requirements. Both buses entered service on 1 May 1954 whereupon some forty-two pre-war Daimler COG5s were taken out of service. (R. Knibbs)

3201 (MOF 201), Daimler CVG6, 18286, Crossley H30/25R, 4/1954

Opposite above: Demonstrating to Chesterfield Corporation in 1954 is 3201 (MOF 201), a new Daimler CVG6 with a Crossley H30/25R body. This bus was delivered to BCT in April 1954 and was sent straight away to demonstrate for Chesterfield. It was operated without its Birmingham municipal crests, although it carried its BCT fleet number. The crew of the bus is approaching 3201 with the look of keen anticipation at the prospect of driving this high-quality vehicle on the 38 route to St Augustines, which is to the south of the town, just west of the main Derby Road. (G. H. F. Atkins)

Four Daimler Fleetlines

3246 (246 DOC)
After 7000 HP had been demonstrated to Birmingham at the end of 1960 and until 31 January 1961 it was returned to Transport Vehicles, who ran it as their demonstrator until 1966. Looking for a second Daimler Fleetline CRG6LX to add to 7000 HP, one of BCT's ten preproduction prototypes (246 DOC) was hired from the municipality during 1962, resulting in these ten Fleetlines being bought on very favourable terms. 3246 had an MCCW H44/33F body, which was completed on 1 February 1962 and looked remarkably similar to 7000 HP. It was finally delivered to Birmingham on 23 July 1962. It was demonstrated to mainly BET Group companies and is working on the 28 service when on loan to North Western Road car in Hempshaw Lane, Stockport, on April Fool's Day 1962. (P. J. Thompson)

3451 (BON 451C)
Overleaf above: Having just been delivered to Tyburn Road Works in March 1965, 3451 (BON 451C) was the very first pioneering Daimler Fleetline CRG6LX single-decker to be built. All subsequent single-deck Fleetlines were classified SRG6LX. 3451 was bodied by Marshall of Cambridge with a B37F layout that was somewhat disappointing as the Fleetlines were bought with the intention of replacing the Leyland PS2/1s, whose seating capacity was only three less. The attractive front of these single-deckers was a contrast to the exposed rear-engined bustle. (L. Mason)

3575 (FOC 575D)

Above left: MCCW-bodied Daimler Fleetline CRG6LX 3575 (FOC 575D) was exhibited and used in service during the British Week in Lyon, France, between 16 October and 5 November 1966. A Birmingham City Transport bus was chosen as Birmingham was twinned with Lyon. It carried advertisements for Lucas, CAV and Girling products between the nearside panels, while on the offside the bus had a complete panel for the British Motor Corporation. The bus could always be identified as it had a small Daimler badge on the centre of the front panel and when in France it had a seating capacity of H41/33F, which was two less than normal. When the bus was in Lyon it had a Union Jack flag attached to the offside above the wing mirror and the French Tricolor on the nearside along with a somewhat dubious route number. 3575 is entering the Rue de la République in the centre of Lyon with the Hôtel de Ville to the right. (W. S. Godden)

3810 (NOV 810G)

Above right: Commercial Motor Shows were always a good place to show off a bus manufacturer's chassis types, bodies or components, but space in the Earls Court Exhibition Halls was always at a premium. Cunning plots were thought up in order to get extra vehicles into the exhibition. Badge engineering had been used in the early 1950s, with AEC using defunct manufacturing company's names such as Crossley and Maudslay to get more vehicles into the show. At the 1968 CMS, 3810 (NOV 810G), a Park Royal H43/29D-bodied Daimler Fleetline CRG6LX, was placed on the Charles Roe stand despite it never having been near the Crossgates factory in Leeds. It is standing alongside a Leeds City Transport double-decker on the Roe stand on 21 September 1968. (K. Walker)

15

Modified Buses: 1953–58

1803 (HOV 803)

Above: After just a year in service, 1803 (HOV 803) was returned to traffic on 8 July 1949 with the proposed new design for the triple-indicator display boxes that were to be introduced on the new-look front buses, whose delivery was to begin during the following year. As a result, 1803 spent the next few years wandering around various garages so that conducting crews could become familiar with the new design. It therefore always looked slightly peculiar – an odd bus out. It is travelling out of the city centre in Hill Street, working on the 15B service to Garretts Green Lane in South Yardley with an old single-track destination blind in the lower box. Against the skyline is the gaunt iron framework of New Street station, which was bombed six times between 16 October 1940 and 28 July 1942 by wartime enemy action. Work would soon begin to demolish it, which took more than three and a half years. (S. N. J. White)

2847 (JOJ 847)

Overleaf above: Perhaps the most radical of all BCT's modified half-cab buses built between 1950 and 1954 was 2847 (JOJ 847), a Crossley-bodied Daimler CVG6. It was involved in a severe accident in Yardley Wood Road and was sent to Midland Red's Carlyle Road Works, where an enclosed BMMO D7-styled platform was fitted. Other modifications included a Cave-Brown-Cave saloon heating system, electrical-operated doors, fluorescent lighting and yellow-painted ceilings. With a H30/25RD layout, 2847 re-entered service on 10 December 1959 and is working on the 9 route in Hagley Road in the following year. (L. Mason)

2856 (JOJ 856)

This bus was not a demonstrator but was equipped with 8-foot-wide axles and wider mudguards as well as just visible lollipop markers – seen to the right of the nearside sidelight. In this condition 2856 (JOJ 856), a Crossley-bodied Daimler CVG6 dating from November 1952, was used in normal service to test the clearances for operating 8-foot-wide buses in Birmingham during 1958. It is at the terminus of the 14 route in Saint Giles Road, Tile Cross. (L. Mason)

2880 (JOJ 880)

As a result of accident damage, two of this class of Crossley-bodied Daimler CVG6s were fitted with the newly introduced concealed radiator developed for Manchester Corporation. It was intended to improve the driver's nearside view and became the standard Daimler CVG6 series front. 2880 (JOJ 880), standing in Tyburn Road Works, has just been fitted with its new all-over blue glass fibre Manchester front, which sat rather uncomfortably on the two buses that received them. (D. R. Harvey Collection)

2926 (JOJ 926)

Above: 2926 (JOJ 926), a Guy Arab IV with a Metro-Cammell body, stands at the 66 terminus in Eachelhurst Road at the junction with Hanson's Bridge Road, just inside city boundary with Sutton Coldfield. The rebuilding of 2926 in July 1956 to a H32/25R seating layout involved a new, steeper two-landing staircase and a blank panel without the staircase window on the offside rear. The bus received a full set of Auster opening front windows, while, uniquely in the fleet, the sliding saloon windows were replaced by pull-in ventilators that each had wind deflectors. (S. N. J. White)

3000 (LOG 301)

Below: They looked the same, but they sounded different! Fitted with a constant mesh gearbox, 3000 (LOG 300) entered service on New Year's Day 1953 as the last of six buses experimentally fitted with this type of manual gearbox for comparison trials with the standard preselector gearboxes usually fitted to these 27-foot-long Guys. They were not easy to drive and were not popular with drivers as they required a lot of skill to handle their gearboxes. They were fitted with a red-knobbed gear lever and all six had a notice in the cab: 'WARNING GEARBOX NOT PRE-SELECTOR. ORDINARY TYPE CLUTCH AND GEARBOX'. 3000 was only a few months old when its driver prepares to pull away from the terminus of the 45 route in Navigation Street. (D. R. Harvey Collection)

Bibliography

The main source of statistical information is the PSV Circle fleet history PD24 (2015), *Birmingham City Transport* and my own *Birmingham Buses at Work, Parts I and II* (Silver Link, 2004 and 2006 respectively). Also, a most valuable source of information was *Road and Rails of Birmingham* by R. T. Coxon (Ian Allan, 1979).

Acknowledgements

The author is grateful to the many photographers acknowledged in the text who have contributed to this volume. Thanks are especially due to Alan Broughall, the late Ray Coxon, John Cull, the late Les Mason, the late Les Perkins, P. Tizard, Jack White and the late Alf Yates, who all allowed me to print all their photographs many years ago and generously gave permission for me to use their material. Where the photographer is not known I have credited them to my own collection.

Special thanks are due to my wife Diana for her support and proofreading and to the continued encouragement given by Connor Stait and Louis Archard at Amberley Publishing.